Mary C. Grey is Emeritus Profes[...] of Wales, Lampeter, a fellow at [...] Professor at St Mary's University C[...] Professor at the University of Winchester. She is also a Patron of Sabeel, an ecumenical grass-roots liberation theology movement among Palestinian Christians, and chairs the Theology Group of Living Stones, which is concerned with the well-being of Christians in the Middle East. She is also the author of many books concerning social justice, including *The Advent of Peace* (SPCK, 2010).

THE RESURRECTION OF PEACE

*A gospel journey to Easter
and beyond*

———✦———

Mary C. Grey

Questions for reflection by Pat Clegg

First published in Great Britain in 2012

Society for Promoting Christian Knowledge
36 Causton Street
London SW1P 4ST
www.spckpublishing.co.uk

British Library Cataloguing-in-Publication Data
A catalogue record for this book is available from the British Library

ISBN 978–0–281–06637–7
eBook ISBN 978–0–281–06638–4

Typeset by Graphicraft Limited, Hong Kong
Manufacture managed by Jellyfish
First printed in Great Britain by CPI Group
Subsequently digitally printed in Great Britain

Produced on paper from sustainable forests

For Nicholas

Contents

———◆•◆———

Acknowledgements

———•◦•———

This book would not have seen the light of day without the encouragement of Philip Law at SPCK, and the work of its editorial team, for which I am genuinely grateful. I am also grateful for this relationship with SPCK, which goes back to the publication of *Redeeming the Dream* in 1989. As with *The Advent of Peace*, I have been greatly helped by the wisdom of Dr Toine van Teeffelen of the Arab Education Institute in Bethlehem, as well as by the advice of Mrs Cedar Duaybis of the board of the Sabeel Ecumenical Liberation Theology Center in Jerusalem. The work of Sabeel in Palestine remains inspirational to me, as do the many Peace Groups both in Palestine, in Israel and here in the UK. It has been a very helpful experience working with the Revd Pat Clegg, who has written the questions for reflection that figure at the end of each chapter, and who offered detailed suggestions along the way from her own experience of leading pilgrimages in the Holy Lands. Nicholas, my husband, has been consistently encouraging and supportive, and shares my commitment to working for peace with justice. I dedicate this book to him in gratitude.

Introduction

To begin a book with a title including both 'resurrection' and 'peace' in itself invites a mood of hope. 'If Christ be not risen then our hope is vain,' wrote St Paul, and this conviction remains central to Christian faith.[1] But hope is not only for joy in eternal life (the ultimate destination), but hope that the kingdom of peace and justice proclaimed by Jesus of Nazareth[2] can be both glimpsed and embodied in our earthly lives now, albeit in imperfect forms. Resurrection hope is to be grounded and experienced in every aspect of our lives – in actions, relationships and lifestyles. And a major grounding of hope has to be sought in wholehearted commitment to peace, to ending conflict, and reconciliation based on justice in troubled and oppressed areas of the world.

A time for hope

As I write,[3] the war in Afghanistan still rumbles on after the killing of Osama Bin Laden, there are conflict-ridden areas in Africa (after a brutal civil war in the Ivory Coast and a catastrophic famine in the Horn of Africa), but in the Middle East generally a new mood emerged in December 2010. Called the Arab Spring, this movement began in Tunisia, followed by uprisings in Egypt, Libya, Syria, Yemen and Bahrain. Each conflict has its own unique character, and it is by no means clear, over a year later, and when the Arab Spring has moved into autumn, winter and another spring is near, whether in every case the outcomes will be positive: freedom for suffering communities. Syria is currently undergoing unspeakable suffering. Every day brings new tensions but also hope. But these ongoing revolutions – in the cases of Tunisia and Egypt, initially, non-violent struggles – are having vast implications for Israel/Palestine. For example, at a conference in 2011 of religious leaders that took place at Lambeth Palace, co-chaired by Archbishop Rowan

Williams and Archbishop Vincent Nichols, these hopeful remarks were made:

> His Beatitude Fouad Twal, Latin Patriarch of Jerusalem, said: 'The recent Arab Spring of youth in the region is spreading ... Sooner or later, with violence or peacefully, it is coming. No regime is immune to these events.'
>
> The Anglican Bishop of Jerusalem, Suheil Dawani, said the Arab Spring demonstrates that 'the people are demanding to be heard' and that as Arab Christians, 'we join our Arab brothers and sisters'.
>
> Dr Bernard Sabella said the Arab Spring reflects the reality that the majority of Arabs want to live 'in an open, preferably secular, democratic society'. That's especially true, he said, for Christians.[4]

Clearly, Israel feels very defensive in the face of Arab unrest as well as political developments in the West Bank and Gaza, especially because the two political parties, Fatah and Hamas,[5] are engaged in a process of reconciliation. When Israel's Prime Minister, Benjamin Netanyahu, visited American President Barack Obama in May 2011, he remained resolute in his opposition to the President's determination to base the forthcoming Palestinian State on the agreed 1967 borders. Whereas this produced deadlock in their discussions in the USA, but hearty approval for Netanyahu back in Israel, there is also a developing critique among certain groups within Israel itself. For example, Gideon Levy, a courageous journalist with the Jerusalem-based liberal paper *Haaretz*, and a long-standing critic of his own government, wrote:

> The 'speech of his life' must now quickly become the speech of Prime Minister Benjamin Netanyahu's political demise. The hour is pressing, there is no time and nothing is going to come of Netanyahu any more. Even the snake oil peddlers who proffered masses of expectations in advance of the speech, who told us that Netanyahu 2 is different from Netanyahu 1, that the man had 'matured', 'internalized', 'grown wiser' and 'become more moderate', that he has learned the lessons of his previous term in office and that we can expect 'sensational surprises' from him – they, too, must now admit the bitter truth. The Israeli Leonid Brezhnev is occupying the Prime Minister's Bureau. A man of yesterday, frozen and rigid, uncompromising, deaf to the sounds of his surroundings and blind to the changing times ...

In the coming days, he might still be able to bask in the warmth of the American legislators' hollow ovations. But once this foam on the surface of the water disperses, the question will arise in full force: What now? Then it will become clear that this prime minister has got us in trouble. Big trouble. We lost the Palestinians a long time ago, and now also the White House's America. Once the speech ended, the chances ended. Before it, we didn't know (ostensibly) where the prime minister was heading. After it, we know the crystal clear answer: nowhere. To some more gained time after which there is nothing, except for increasing dangers and a chance missed once again.

Now it is certain: Netanyahu will go down in the history of Israel and of the world as a forgotten footnote.[6]

Clearly, this is a highly controversial view, and definitely not reflected by Israel as a whole, yet I take it as one indicator of the ferment in the Middle East and the yearning of its peoples for change. Even if American opinion remains solidly backing Israel (apart from some human rights groups), there are signs that European opinion has shifted: for example, *The Guardian*, in an article, 'Europe's Israel romance is on the wane', pointed out that Europeans are losing their illusions about Israel. Policy is now out of step with the public opinion:

In Europe, Israel has historically enjoyed a high level of support, not least because it was perceived as a progressive democracy in a sea of Arab backwardness. At the same time, most Europeans knew very little about the Israel–Palestine conflict. As recently as 2004, the Glasgow University Media Group found that only 9 per cent of British students knew that the Israelis were the illegal occupiers of Palestinian land. Astonishingly, there were actually more people (11 per cent) who believed that the Palestinians were occupying the territories.

However, according to a new poll by ICM for the *Middle East Monitor*, Europeans' perception of Israel has changed decisively, and their understanding of the Israel–Palestine conflict, while still giving some cause for concern, has improved significantly. The survey of 7,000 people in Germany, France, Spain, Italy, the Netherlands and Britain revealed that only a small minority (10 per cent) now believe their countries should support Israel rather than the Palestinians, while many more, 39 per cent, think they should not.

This shift in European public opinion may owe something to an improved understanding of the conflict . . . This persistence of ignorance about issues that have been long established in international law may reflect media bias, or inadequate coverage of the conflict. It could also be a result of campaigns undertaken by the Israeli public relations machinery in Europe. Whatever the cause, the shift in public opinion is clearly not mainly due to the success of a pro-Palestinian lobby.

This decisive shift appears to be primarily a consequence of Israel's violation of international law, specifically in its actions in Gaza, the 2010 attack on the humanitarian flotilla, its settlement expansion programme, and the construction of the separation wall.

There is, across Europe, a growing rejection of Israeli policies [the writer does not refer here to the USA] . . . While it is important to note that those polled saw fault on both sides, 31 per cent considered Palestinians to be the primary victims of the conflict, while only 6 per cent thought Israelis the primary victims . . .

European policy on Palestine can no longer be said to reflect the values and aspirations of the people. The survey confirms a disturbing level of disconnect between public opinion and governments' actions. Whereas the EU took a decision in 2003 to place Hamas on its list of terrorist organizations and preclude it from any negotiations, 45 per cent of those polled said it should be included in peace talks, while only 25 per cent said it should be excluded. (A recent survey by the Institute for Jewish Policy research also found that 52 per cent of British Jews support negotiating with Hamas for peace.)

[. . .]

The results of this study coincide with the epic changes now engulfing the Middle East.

[. . .]

[Israel's] twentieth-century image as the battling underdog in a hostile neighbourhood has been shattered by its actions. European governments should bring their policies into line with universally accepted human values. Anything less will be a betrayal of the democratic standards Europe claims to uphold.[7]

In addition, and perhaps a consequence of these far-reaching political changes, Egypt has now opened the Rafah crossing into Gaza, closed since Israel's incursion into Gaza in 2009. It is hoped this will bring relief to the long suffering of the people of Gaza, effectively blocked off from the world in an ever-worsening poverty.

Christian Churches in the Arab Spring?

But how are Christians faring in the Arab Spring? A mixed picture is appearing. There has been a long process – growing in its proportions – of Christians leaving the Middle East. Robert Fisk, writing from Lebanon a few months before the Arab Spring, speaks of an 'exodus that almost reaches biblical proportions':[8]

> Across the Middle East, it is the same story of despairing – sometimes frightened – Christian minorities . . . Almost half of Iraq's Christians have fled their country since the Gulf War of 1991, most of them after the 2004 invasion – a weird tribute to the faith of the two Bush presidents who went to war with Iraq – and stand now at 550,000, scarcely 3 per cent of the population. More than half of Lebanon's Christians live outside the country. Once a majority, the nation's one and a half million Christians, most of them Maronite Catholics, comprise perhaps 35 per cent of the Lebanese. Egypt's Coptic Christians – there are at most eight million – now represent less than 10 per cent of the population.

Less than three months after this was written, Coptic Christians in Egypt[9] on New Year's Eve 2010 were attacked by Islamic fundamentalists in the Coptic Orthodox Church in the city of Alexandria. Twenty-one people were killed and many more injured. On 30 January, a few days after the demonstrations to reform the Egyptian government, Muslims in southern Egypt broke into two homes belonging to Coptic Christians. These Muslim assailants murdered eleven people and wounded four others. Yet such brutal killings have to be contrasted with other facts: in Tahrir Square, Cairo, on Wednesday 2 February 2011, Coptic Christians joined hands to provide a protective cordon around their Muslim neighbours during *salah* (prayers) amid the 2011 Egyptian Revolution. For Iraqi Christians, the continuing spectre of growing insecurity, especially the rise of radical Islam, which has led to church bombings, kidnappings and assassinations, has created a situation that has caused them to leave in large numbers. Perhaps as many as 300,000 have left Iraq, never to return. Others are refugees in the region: in recent years some 150,000 in Syria and possibly up to 40,000 in Jordan.[10]

Fisk sees the tensions at their greatest in Jerusalem:

Nowhere is the Christian fate sadder than in the territories around Jerusalem. As Monsignor Fouad Twal, the ninth Latin patriarch of Jerusalem, and the second to be an Arab, put it bleakly, 'The Israelis regard us as 100 per cent Palestinian Arabs and we are oppressed in the same way as the Muslims. But Muslim fundamentalists identify us with the Christian West – which is not always true – and want us to pay the price.'[11]

Anthony O'Mahony has described the entire twentieth century as a period of conflict, which did not leave the Churches of the Middle East untouched.[12] There had been a long history of Churches' refusal to recognize each other:

It was not until the nineteenth century that reformist measures allowed these ancient Churches to be formally recognized. Modern crisis and contemporary ecumenism are beginning to bring down the barriers. In the course of the last decades, remarkable developments have taken place in the ecumenical relations between Churches in the Middle East, both on bilateral and multilateral levels – agreements that allow partial mutual participation in sacraments, formation of future priests, and catechesis.[13]

He identifies three main factors responsible for these positive developments: the ecumenical movement of the twentieth century and the establishment (in 1948) of the World Council of Churches, the Second Vatican Council, and the large-scale emigration from the Middle East to Europe, the Americas and Australia. The emigration, described in Robert Fisk's article as a 'biblical-style exodus', has had the positive consequences of enabling publication without censorship, and has brought the existence of the non-Chalcedonian Churches more into the awareness of the western Churches, providing an opportunity and incentive for theological dialogue. Sadly, Christian communities have inevitably lost many of their young and most educated members, part of their future and potential leadership. O'Mahony concludes:

Christianity originated in the Middle East. The Christian presence there today bears witness to the global Church of the unity of its origins and the diversity of its expression. Christians also help maintain and sustain the diversity in the Middle East. However, there has been a large-scale flight from the Middle East and this has implications for those left behind. Christianity in the Middle East has a witness beyond itself: let us hope that the Churches of East and West rise rapidly to this challenge, for the key to the future of this important region may lie with the few.[14]

So it is unclear how the Arab Spring will affect Christianity in the long run. Continuing violence in Syria shows no sign of ending. As O'Mahony wrote in December 2011:

With so much at stake, Syria, its neighbours both friendly and hostile, and the wider Middle Eastern region are at a crossroad, where the optimistic breezes of the Arab spring have turned into chilling winter winds propelled by colliding pressure systems of ideology, strategic relations and sectarian division.[15]

Clearly, Christians are an important presence in the Bible lands: they are an integral part of their origins, ongoing dynamic and future hope.

The Lenten pilgrimage to Easter

This book, like my last one, to which this is a companion and follow up,[16] focuses on 'the resurrection of peace' in Israel/Palestine as well as the wider context of Christians in the Bible lands – Syria, Lebanon and Egypt – whose existence is threatened by the conflicts.

The previous book ended with the shepherds crying, after their visit to Bethlehem, that their real journey was now beginning.[17] There, the focus of the Advent journey to peace began in Bethlehem; here, the Lenten journey to peace begins by the Sea of Galilee and follows Jesus' journey to Jerusalem – and then back to Galilee, post-resurrection. It will be a pilgrimage in many senses. Pilgrimages in all faiths are times for reflection and spiritual renewal and are often associated with sacred places, like Mecca for Muslims, Buddha's birthplace in Varanasi (India) for Buddhists, the golden Temple of Amritsar for Sikhs, Canterbury, Assisi, Rome, Ephesus or Jerusalem for Christians. Sacred springs, mountains, rocks and trees may be involved. Christian Lenten pilgrimages are associated with asceticism, with 'giving up' some luxury item like chocolates or alcohol – but more recently there has been a move to re-examine and practise asceticism in a more transformative direction. This can mean a focus on deeper prayer, a rekindling of faith through the re-examination of lifestyle and values and a commitment to action. The journey may also be accompanied by conversion experiences, a new 'seeing' and a transformation of ethical principles. Creation-centred ecological groups focus on the Lenten pilgrimage as time for conversion to the earth, to more earth-friendly actions and lifestyles. Others seek stillness and a more contemplative way of living, resisting pressures to be forever busy, the temptation to superficiality and consumerist competitiveness.

The pilgrimage embarked on here may include all these aspects: it revisits the sacred places in the land called holy by Christians, Jews and Muslims. It has been a cherished destination for pilgrimages since at least the fourth century, as we know from the journeys of the female pilgrim, Egeria, who spent a lengthy stay in the Holy Lands, especially in Jerusalem, from 381–4 CE.[18] Egeria wrote down her observations in a letter now called *Itinerarium Egeriae*, or the *Travels of Egeria*. Her writings are a useful tool because she describes the monks, many holy places and geographical points in her travels, and even the early details of the liturgical practices of the church at Jerusalem.

Pilgrimages may involve a sense of the unknown, a sense of expectation and discovery. Even if, as T. S. Eliot so memorably wrote, the result is to return to one's home and know it 'for the first time',[19] life and relationships may be transformed, sometimes in very dramatic ways.[20] One of the issues with pilgrimages in Israel/Palestine is that current tour operators may treat them as mere holidays, as tourist excursions, ignoring the fact that tourism has serious ethical dimensions. At last travellers have begun to understand that this is an important factor in visits to many developing countries, where tourists may stay in luxury hotels, with food imported from their own home countries, with little or no benefit to the host country – but this awareness is often not present in the Holy Land. One of the reasons for this is the political situation, where Israel and the Israeli Tourist Board attempt to control pilgrimages by making it difficult for Palestinian guides to become authorized, thus controlling visits through their own guides. Incursions into the West Bank are strictly controlled – sometimes eliminating Bethlehem and Bethany completely from the itinerary (except, perhaps, a minimal stop in Manger Square to see the Church of the Nativity), so tourists and pilgrims are unable to make contact with Palestinians, hear their stories or gain insights into their true situation. A recent initiative in Palestine, PIRT,[21] has now offered an ethical code of conduct for pilgrimages. It recognizes that encountering the 'living stones' of Palestine, as well as the revered ancient ones, is an important part of the pilgrimage experience. Meeting with local communities, worshipping with them in their local churches, appreciating their culture – dance, story, song and food – enriches the pilgrimage experience. Nor should this be one-sided: entering into the faith experiences of the three Abrahamic faiths with reverence, trying to understand the history and aspirations of three peoples in their religious and political contexts, can be a transforming experience. But this does raise the question of how we should read the sacred texts.

How are we to read the sacred texts?

Daily readings of Scripture are part and parcel of Christian life and become even more significant during a pilgrimage. Even if reading the Bible may be supplemented by other texts, by inspiring writings of saints, Desert Fathers and Mothers, poets (ancient and modern), the Bible will always hold a special place, especially when we attempt in some way from the distance of more than 2,000 years to follow the footsteps of Christ and revisit sites where Christian discipleship seeks to re-source itself.

As the above sections have shown, the Holy Lands, parts of which are under occupation by the Israeli government, are places of acute suffering for the Arab population. Yet we come to the Bible often leaving this knowledge in the background, frequently unaware of the existence of our presuppositions, the lenses through which we read the text, influenced by our church backgrounds, age, gender and position in society. Scripture includes many different types of texts – with genres as far apart as poetry, proverbs, hymns of praise and lament, and ethical exhortations. Even when the texts appear to be historical, they are written at a particular period, for a particular purpose. When it comes to the four Christian Gospels it is now recognized that these were written by the evangelists, for specific communities with their own needs and questions. But the answers to their problems and questions may not be the answers we seek for our own: even our questions will differ and may not be sufficiently articulated. The Bible does not directly address the burning issues of today: Jesus does not give any advice on contraception; nor does he address the question of the ordination of women.

So it is vital to recognize that we read the texts through certain lenses – there is no view from nowhere.[22] For example, ecological groups may read texts through a lens that encourages positive views on creation. Feminist biblical scholars comb the texts to uncover affirmative attitudes to women. Liberation readings read texts condemning riches and power and focus on passages urging justice for the poor. Post-colonial readings seek to find a congruity between their own resistance to empire and that of the Bible. We may be using several lenses at the same time. The danger in each case is that of bringing a predetermined conviction of a particular issue and claiming that this is the 'true message of the Bible'. This stance is often adopted by a Church or denomination to justify its own stance. It is of vital importance when confronted with the claims of Jewish and Christian Zionism that the land belongs to Israel, because 'the Bible says so'.

Briefly, Christian Zionism co-operates with the interests of Jewish Zionism by agreeing that for the Second Coming of Christ, the Jewish people must have returned to Israel and be in possession of the land. This was a growing movement in the nineteenth century, involving a coalescing of aims between Christian evangelicals like Lord Shaftesbury, and early Jewish Zionists like Theodore Herzl: culminating in the Balfour declaration of 1917, promising a home for the Jewish People, its triumph was the UN declaration of 1947 – that the state of Israel would be that home.

The Jewish Zionist Movement, though originally secular in character, now relies heavily on a literalist reading of Scripture in which God gives the Jewish people the Promised Land, now identified with the state of Israel, but arguably with territories stretching from the land of the two rivers (Tigris and Euphrates) to Sinai. But such a reading ignores the fact that at the time of successive waves of Jewish people arriving into Palestine – both pre- and post-1948 – it was not a case of their arrival into 'a land without a people for a people without a land' (Lord Shaftesbury's phrase), but of their shock on discovering that this land was already inhabited by the Palestinian people, with their rich culture and traditions, and had been for centuries.

This means both that there cannot be simply one reading of the text, but multiple readings; that, in the pilgrim journey, we listen with expectation for new understandings as we balance the many voices and many interpretations. And in all things we trust the inspiration of the Holy Spirit, leading us ever forward to a greater depth of truth and justice.

Threatened with resurrection?

The pilgrim journey is not undertaken without anxiety or even fear. Fear of change brings insecurity; surrendering presuppositions and old certainties appears threatening. In a certain sense, we can speak, like the Guatemalan poet Julia Esquivel, of being *threatened with resurrection*. Here she speaks of overcoming fears – in her case, the sufferings of the civil war in her country.

> I am no longer afraid of death,
> I know well
> its dark and cold corridors
> leading to life.
>
> I am afraid rather of that life
> which does not come out of death,
> which cramps our hands
> and retards our march.
>
> I am afraid of my fear
> and even more of the fear of others,
> who do not know where they are going,
> who continue clinging
> to what they think is life
> which we know to be death!

> I live each day to kill death;
> I die each day to give birth to life,
> and in this death of death,
> I die a thousand times
> and am reborn another thousand
> through that love
> from my People,
> which nourishes hope![23]

It is this dynamic of death and rebirth, the Easter transformation, the hope that is both seed and yeast for Christian living, that is explored in this book.

1

The sea of challenge

———•◦•———

> O Sabbath rest by Galilee!
> O calm of hills above,
> where Jesus knelt to share with Thee,
> the silence of eternity,
> interpreted by love.[1]

This beautiful Sea, ringed by the hills of Galilee and the Golan Heights, sparkles before our eyes: this is the Lenten journey's beginning, simply because Galilee is the main setting for Jesus' ministry, as related by all four Gospels.[2] It is also the place Jesus commanded his disciples to return to, after the resurrection. Whereas Bethlehem and the West Bank were the focus of my previous book, *The Advent of Peace*,[3] Galilee is now the beacon calling us with its own story, then and now. We do not know why Jesus chose to leave Nazareth and go to the shores of Galilee, to work among poor fisherfolk and agricultural workers, making journeys to Jerusalem for the feasts and then 'set his face to go to Jerusalem' for the final confrontation with the ruling powers.[4] It is possible that Galilee offered easy access to the Gentile world – Jesus seems to have moved easily to non-Jewish situations and back again.

Our path here will, first, revisit the holy places revered for memories of Jesus' ministry; second, look at the political and historical context of Galilee now that cries out for peace; and third, revisit the political and theological purposes of Jesus in his own journey that would lead to death followed by resurrection.

Galilee of the nations (Isaiah 9.1) – the sacred sites

In Roman times this country was divided into Judea, Samaria and Galilee, which comprised the whole northern section of the country and was the largest of the three regions. Herod Antipas, son of Herod the Great, ruled Galilee as tetrarch.[5]

The pilgrim visiting the Sea of Galilee for the first time is struck simply by its beauty. The Sea of Galilee (sometimes called the Lake of Tiberias) is about 21 kilometres long and 12 kilometres wide.[6] Because it is 200 metres below sea level it has a climate all of its own: it is subtropical for most of the year, yet storms may develop quickly – as the Gospel stories tell us dramatically. Most of Galilee consists of rocky terrain, between 500 and 700 metres high. There are several high mountains in Galilee, including the Mount of Transfiguration, Mount Tabor[7] and Mount Meron,[8] which have relatively low temperatures and high rainfall.[9] As a result of this climate, flora and wildlife thrive in the region – some are unique to the area – while many birds annually migrate from colder climates to Africa and back through the Hula–Jordan corridor. The streams and waterfalls – waterfalls mainly in upper Galilee – along with vast fields of greenery and colourful wild flowers, including cyclamen, peonies and rhododendron, as well as numerous towns of biblical importance, make the region popular to tourists and pilgrims alike. Alongside this evocative picture, a more negative feature intrudes, namely that the level of water of the Sea of Galilee – like the Dead Sea – has dropped considerably in recent years. This is due not only to drought but to excessive use of water:

> In 1964 Israel completed the National Water Carrier – a phenomenal project that carries water from Lake Kinneret[10] to the Negev. But the water usage has increased drastically across the nation due to the enormous influx of immigrants into the state of Israel and the developments that have taken place across the land. Today there is a shortfall annually of 50 million cubic metres between the amount of water that is taken from the Sea of Galilee, and that which is replenished by the water sources in the Golan Heights.[11]

Another sadness is that Palestinian fishermen are no longer allowed to fish in the lake's waters: Israeli boats now control the fishing industry. In addition, the 'Jesus boats' – tourist/pilgrim boats working the Sea of Galilee – now all fly the Israeli flag.[12] The theme and reality of water supply in Israel/Palestine will continually recur in this book as a great source of suffering. Indisputably, water is a key feature of Middle Eastern conflict today.

Around the Sea of Galilee are many towns and villages of ancient Canaanite origin. Josephus, the first-century Jewish historian, mentions 204 villages. Jesus, on his way from Nazareth, would have passed through Sepphoris (Zippori), once the capital of Galilee until that title passed to the newly constructed Tiberias founded by Herod Antipas in 20 CE, both as a resort and as a stronghold. (It is possible that Joseph, the father of Jesus, went to Sepphoris as a construction worker, accompanied by the boy Jesus.) After reaching the high road, the Via Maris, he would pass Gennesaret and come to Heptapegon (the Seven Springs), the fishing ground for Capernaum's fisherfolk. Heptapegon would later be shortened by Arab speakers to 'Tabgha'. Bargil Pixner, the late Benedictine scholar who spent so much time in the monastery at Tabgha, tells us that here, in winter and early spring, the tropical fish that feel the cold – especially Peter's fish – are attracted by the warm waters of the springs and become an easy catch for fishermen.

Jesus would then arrive at Capernaum: here, among humble peasant people, he chose his base for most of his ministry. It becomes his own town. Capernaum was a frontier town with a population of about 1,500, a mixed community of Jews and Gentiles, people who had long suffered the effects of the Roman Empire, as we shall explore later. Mystery surrounds the character of Capernaum – a hotbed of unrest or economic protest? A small garrison was stationed here that protected the frontier and provided back-up for the tax collectors. The custom house of Matthew, the tax collector, stood near where the Via Maris passed close to the lake.[13] Capernaum had also been on the crossroads of a trade route between Egypt and Syria. Not far away in the hills were the hidden Zealot strongholds – we know that at least one of Jesus' apostles was a Zealot.[14] Now long ruined, Capernaum lies peacefully on the edge of the Sea.[15] But it is not difficult through the excavations of what may have been Peter's house, the first-century synagogue – whose basalt block foundations belonged to the synagogue restored by the centurion mentioned in the Gospels[16] – and customs buildings to imagine life in New Testament times.

That this was an area significant for pilgrimage is shown by the fact that the earliest woman pilgrim on record, Egeria (referred to in the Introduction), visited Capernaum and Tabgha and tells of a cave in the hillside at the Seven Springs. She relates that the Lord ascended above and preached the Beatitudes that we know as the Sermon on the Mount:[17]

> The terrace above this still existing cave, called Mughara Ayub, must be considered the traditional place of the Sermon on the Mount. The hillcrest of Eremos (= the desert place) indeed offers a magnificent view over the entire lake and the surrounding villages.[18]

Wherever it is decided was the authentic site for the Sermon on the Mount, it is the Mount of the Beatitudes that points to the heart of the purpose of this book. For our pilgrimage is not merely to follow the footsteps of Jesus insofar as these can be reconstructed but to make his message our own, in the struggle for the peace and justice of the kingdom in our own time. To visit Capernaum, Tabgha – the Church of the Loaves and Fishes and other sites by the lake, like the Church of the Primacy of Peter[19] – or Tiberias is almost like being pulled by an invisible thread to the Mount of the Beatitudes, simply because the Beatitudes' message has been recognized through the centuries as being Jesus' legacy to us in the struggle for peace. Today's Melkite Archbishop of Galilee, Elias Chacour, refers in his many works to the pull of this mountain in his life.[20] As a small boy he would take refuge here, for the presence of Christ was tangible – as the hymn of the Quaker poet, Whittier, cited at the head of this chapter, tried to evoke. There is a rich legacy of inspiration for today's Peace Movement, from the way Leo Tolstoy was influenced by the Beatitudes and how this impacted on Gandhi and then Martin Luther King. Gandhi read the Sermon on the Mount every day and it was also prayed by the community in his ashrams. The Jesuit peace activist, John Dear, describes dramatically how his own quest for peace was inspired by reading the Beatitudes on the Mount:

> I hiked past the ruins of Capernaum, through the green fields, and up a steep hill to a stone church adorned with arches and columns. It was surrounded by palm trees, cacti, and shrubs and overlooked the sea. This was the Chapel of the Beatitudes.[21]

John Dear began to read the Beatitudes inscribed on the windows of the chapel, and recalled other parts of the Sermon, on which he had been meditating. Suddenly he began to feel the words were addressed to him personally:

> And then, I suddenly released, *Oh, my God, I think Jesus is serious!* My knees went rubbery, my jaw dropped, and my mouth went dry. I walked onto the balcony to puzzle things over. I gazed at the panorama before me – the deepness of the sea, the mountains in the distance, the vivid green of the hills and the sky an improbable blue – all of it visible and real from where I stood . . . *What does this mean? Is this what I'm called to be – actually and truly? Meek and mournful? Merciful and poor in spirit? To hunger for justice and make peace?*[22]

Stunned, he asks God for a sign:

> At that moment, a deafening roar split the air. I jumped back, ducked, and scanned the horizon in the direction of the thunder. Then I saw them – two Israeli fighter jets falling out of the blue, rocketing across the sea, mere yards above the water, breaking the sound barrier and setting off sonic booms – and heading right toward me. I thought they might fly into the balcony where I crouched, but at the last instant they pulled up, and blasted over the chapel.[23]

In fact, the jets dropped their bombs in Lebanon and John Dear committed himself to dedicating the rest of his life to living out the Beatitudes – *and never asking for a sign again!* And this is the first reason for calling this initial chapter 'The sea of challenge': the inspiration and mission of the Beatitudes are interwoven with Jesus' own passion for justice and peace as he traversed the Sea and journeyed through its adjacent villages – offering a leitmotiv in the pilgrimage of this book. The next step is to explore Galilee's history and political context today – the setting for the pilgrimage. It will lead us into another area of challenge.

The suffering of Galilee today

In the early twentieth century, when Palestine was still under the Ottoman Empire, followed by the British Mandate, Galilee was inhabited by Arab Christians and Muslims, the Druze,[24] and Jews, while minorities from elsewhere in the Ottoman Empire – including Circassians and Bosniaks – were also settled here by the Turks. Two Circassian villages still exist in the Galilee region today. From the nineteenth century Zionist immigrants had slowly begun to inhabit the land. Once the state of Israel was declared as the new homeland for the Jews in 1948, things changed drastically for indigenous inhabitants through what the Arabs call *Al-Nakba* – the catastrophe. The facts are easy to relate but they may obscure the profundity of the tragedy that was inflicted on the Palestinians and continues to haunt them to this day. The Arab inhabitants of Palestine were driven out of 531 villages by Israeli soldiers; about 750,000 people were displaced, forced into becoming refugees in Bethlehem, Lebanon, Syria and the rest of the world.[25] We are told that:

> Palestinian refugees generally fall into three main groups: Palestinian refugees displaced in 1948, internally displaced Palestinians who remained within the areas that became the state of Israel, and Palestinian refugees displaced in 1967 from the West Bank and Gaza Strip. For the past 58 years, Israel has continued to deny Palestinian refugees their right to return to their ancestral towns, villages and homes ...
>
> Palestinians are the largest and longest suffering group of refugees in the world. One in three refugees worldwide is Palestinian. There are about 7.2 million Palestinian refugees worldwide. More than 4.3 million Palestinian refugees and their descendants displaced in 1948 are registered for humanitarian assistance with the United Nations. Another 1.7 million Palestinian refugees and their descendants, also displaced in 1948, are not registered with the UN. About 355,000 Palestinians and their descendants are internally displaced i.e. inside present-day 'Israel'. When the West Bank and Gaza Strip were occupied in 1967, the UN reported that approximately 200,000 Palestinians fled their homes. These 1967 refugees and their descendants today number about 834,000 persons. As a result of house demolition, revocation of residency rights and construction of illegal settlements on confiscated Palestinian-owned land, at least 57,000 Palestinians have become internally displaced in the occupied West Bank. This number includes 15,000 people so far displaced by the construction of Israel's Annexation Wall. Such dispossession of the Palestinian population continues today.[26]

This version of events is disputed by the Zionist government: it is frequently said that 'they went away, leaving the houses and buildings empty'.[27] Jewish settlers are not told the truth of the empty houses to which they are assigned on arrival from many European countries. The very word *Nakba* was ordered to be erased from school textbooks, its veracity denied. If the Holocaust is claimed as the defining event of Jewish identity today, *Al-Nakba* must be one of its equivalents in Arab memory.

When Sabeel's international conference in 2008 decided to focus on *Al-Nakba* (at its fortieth anniversary), participants were told personal stories by those who had experienced the catastrophe. The founder and director of Sabeel, the Revd Naim Ateek, together with his brothers and sisters, took some of us to the site of his own former village, Beisan. Elias Chacour, now Archbishop of Galilee, has poignantly documented his boyhood experiences of expulsion.[28] Yet each village has its own stories, its own inhabitants with their memories.[29] One witness writes:

> The new rulers have moved into our lands, our homes, claiming them as their own. The great promises of our brother nations and of the world are forgotten. We flee or are driven out of our homes and families. We wander, exiled. Many families seek refuge in neighbouring lands or distant countries, but many of us become refugees in our own land – squatting in tent camps as we watch our land, our home become home to another people.[30]

When the moment came to visit these villages I was apprehensive. Our coach sped along the highway at the foot of Mount Carmel, densely planted with trees – a sign, we were told, that Arab villages had once existed here. Of all the places visited, I have chosen to tell the story of one village with a particularly painful history. This is Al Tantura, on the coast south of Haifa. Arriving here on a warm sunny day, standing on the golden sand by the sparkling blue-green sea (with one ruined stone house on the shore), it is scarcely credible to believe that on 23 May 1948, a week after the state of Israel was declared, the Alexandroni Brigade captured Al Tantura. Originally it was thought that the village fell 'after a brief battle'.[31] But the MA thesis of Teddy Katz of Haifa University tells a different story. He argues that a massacre of between 200 and 250 people occurred – the parking lot by the entrance to the beach serves as a mass grave. According to Muhammad Abu Hana, a former resident:

> after the battle, the residents were rounded up on the beach, where the men were separated from the women ... On the beach, soldiers led groups of men away, and you could hear gunfire after each departure. Toward noon we were led on foot to an orchard to the east of the village, and I saw bodies piled on a cart pulled by men of Tantura who emptied their cargo in a big pit. Then trucks arrived, and women and children were loaded onto them and driven to Furaydis. On the road, near the railroad tracks, other bodies were scattered about.[32]

After all remaining residents had been expelled, the village was completely demolished, except for the house on the beach we were now looking at, and an adjacent Muslim shrine. Four weeks later, the village site was resettled and a kibbutz established. This same site is now a popular recreational area.

The story of Al Tantura – out of many other possible stories – is retold here for several reasons. In *The Advent of Peace* I told the story of Joseph Ben-Eleazer, who played a part in this massacre, as well as in the expulsion of the village of Lod, but who subsequently became a Christian and sought forgiveness from one of the families he had wronged.[33] So the story goes on. But there are further repercussions. It was very difficult for the MA student, Teddy Katz, to get his study accepted. Once the Israeli authorities became aware of what was written, his evidence was denied, and the thesis was declared to have failed, despite being originally awarded a distinction by the university. The student's supervisor, Professor Ilan Pappé, fought for justice through the Israeli courts and a Commission of Inquiry, risking his reputation and career.[34] Teddy Katz has never been completely vindicated; Pappé's own relationship with the University of Haifa eventually became intolerable – despite overwhelming support from international academics. So this village's story is illustrative of the difficulty of recovering and maintaining the truth of events in 1948. It is also a warning as to the sophisticated techniques employed to destroy collective memory and identity.

Now, 63 years on, *Al-Nakba* is still firmly enshrined in Palestinian collective memory (in Israel, Gaza and the West Bank), despite some evidence that some of the younger generation have a diminished attachment to their ancestral village. Nakba Day – 15 May – is still celebrated by the villagers and many international supporters, with pilgrimages to the old sites and non-violent resistance marches to checkpoints and other places of significance. But remembering *Al-Nakba* is one thing; living as second-class citizens, as a minority within a Jewish state, is another.[35]

There are about one and a half million Palestinians living within the borders of the Israeli state.[36] Arab citizens of Israel form a majority of the population (52 per cent) in Israel's Northern District and about 50 per cent of the Arab population lives in 114 different localities throughout Israel. In total there are 122 primarily, if not entirely, Arab localities in Israel, 89 of them having populations over 2,000. Some 46 per cent of Israel's Arab population (622,400 people) lives in predominantly Arab communities in the north, Nazareth being the largest Arab city, with a population of 65,000, roughly 40,000 of whom are Muslim. Jerusalem has the largest overall Arab population. In 2000, Jerusalem housed 209,000 Arabs, and they make up some 33 per cent of the city's residents. But these facts do little to convey the realities faced by Arab Israelis, who face discrimination, racism and poverty on a daily basis. Almost 140,000 Palestinian families in Israel are below the poverty line – more than 50 per cent of Palestinian children live in these poor families.[37] Poverty now reaches into the third generation. Around 60 per cent of Palestinian families suffer from housing shortages, but 44 per cent cannot afford to rent or purchase a new house or apartment. Permits to build are almost impossible to get – hence the often desperate act of building without a permit, with the frequent consequence of the house being demolished by the Israeli authorities. This is well documented by Jeff Halper, the founder of the Israeli Committee against House Demolitions (ICAHD).[38] Thousands of demolitions have been carried out over the years, under the aegis of five government bodies. The underlying purpose is to 'de-Arabize the land':

> The purpose is to confine the 3.7 million Palestinians of the Occupied territories, together with the 1.3 million Palestinian citizens of Israel, to small, disconnected enclaves (referred to by Sharon as 'cantons') on about 15 per cent of the entire country.[39]

But the overarching plan of ridding the Jewish state of Arabs is given a cloak of legality: demolitions are couched within dry, technical, seemingly neutral master plans. Prime Minister Netanyahu called Arab citizens a demographic problem. Avigdor Lieberman, Deputy Prime Minister, has called for the execution of the Arab members of the Knesset, and supports the idea of the forcible transfer of the Arab community.[40]

Wherever we look, Arab Israelis suffer discrimination, with high unemployment, poor health care and under-representation in Parliament – and a desperate sense of insecurity, heightened by the consciousness that Israel is demanding an acceptance from all citizens that this will be a Jewish state. This is the context for the contemporary search for peace.[41]

Galilee: the sea of challenge for us today

We are again by the shores of the Sea of Galilee at the end of a Sabeel conference. Again the waters are gleaming. Like the 5,000 who shared bread and fish at the time of Jesus, we share the bread of Eucharist, sobered by what we have learnt and the gravity of the task ahead. Yet as Naim Ateek reminds us, the Jesus movement was very small in its origins. Jesus spoke of being salt and light. 'To be salt is to effect change, and the change we seek is the transformation of society.' We seek it with integrity and truth and with the Sabeel (= way) of faithfulness to the gospel.

In the light of the present realities, how shall we reread the sacred texts to inspire the pilgrim journey? Here, almost in the shadow of the Mount of the Beatitudes, with the words 'Blessed are the Peacemakers' ringing in our ears, can we avoid the centrality of the message of peace in the Gospels, and hold it relevant today in the pilgrim journey to Easter? A growing number of biblical scholars[42] now understand the Jesus movement as a movement of resistance to the Roman Empire and for the transformation of this regime of violence and oppression into an alternative society of justice, peace, forgiveness and love. For example, Ched Myers thinks that this is *exactly* the reason Jesus came to Capernaum by the Sea, with its 17 fishing villages, to begin his ministry.[43] Go where the pain is felt the most, Myers asserts. So it is no surprise, given Jesus' compassion for the misery of the fisher-folk (and we can imagine he himself had earned money mending nets), that the call of Matthew to be part of the movement happens so soon. Matthew (Levi) had probably sold fishing rights to the people and charged interest on his services. So he would be the representative at street level of the Roman system. His conversion is a reminder to us that Jesus called both poor and rich. Nor is it a mere decorative symbol to choose the fish as Christianity's earliest emblem: the gospel call has both economic and social dimensions.[44] The fishing industry was for the poor of this region the public face of the injustice of the Roman Empire.

Tragically, far too often do we read *out* of the text of the Gospels their call to peace with justice as the central message of the kingdom. What did Mark do in the first chapter of his Gospel (Mark 1.14) but proclaim the good news of the kingdom and call for a change of heart (*metanoia*)? And what is the good news exactly? It is the proclamation that the kingdom of God is a kingdom of peace and justice, and is offered by God as alternative to the Roman Empire with its Pax Romana.[45] Why have we become so deaf to the fact that peace is the major theme of the New Testament? Is it because it would demand too much of us today?

In his wonderful study of this theme, *Covenant of Peace: The Missing Peace in New Testament Theology and Ethics*,[46] Willard M. Swartley points out that Jesus stands directly in the prophetic tradition of 'shalom' of Isaiah and the other prophets. (It is no accident that Isaiah functions almost as a fifth Gospel.[47]) But shalom does not mean simply 'peace', but the kind of well-being and flourishing that is based upon justice and a quality of right relation permeating society. This meaning persisted in rabbinic Judaism from the second century to the medieval period. What is important is that there was an *ethical category* to shalom that is frequently missed:

> *shalom* primarily signifies a value, an *ethical category* – it denotes the over-coming of strife, quarrel, and social tension, the prevention of enmity and war . . . The pursuit of peace is the obligation of the individual and the goal of various social regulations and structures.[48]

23

Have we forgotten this ethical quality of 'shalom' and thus pushed the centrality of peacemaking to the edges of our consciousness, or to an individualized notion of contentment? The Roman Empire has long fallen but others have risen to take its place. The waters of Galilee have watched the Ottoman Empire, British and Jordanian powers come and go, but the might of the Israelis backed by the Americans, the lack of moral tone and any element of justice in the so-called Peace Process, means that the current situation is strikingly similar to the days when Jesus offered poor fisherfolk and farm labourers an alternative to the regime of the occupier. This is where the Lenten journey begins – with a response to the sea of challenge. But our next step will be to follow Jesus to the desert of temptation.

Questions for reflection

1   Sitting on the shores of the Sea of Galilee is a political act. In Jesus' day the Roman garrison at Capernaum was a daily reminder of life lived under an oppressive regime. Take some time to reread the Beatitudes (Matthew 5.1–12), if possible reading them aloud, hearing them as though for the first time. How does that reading equate with your previous experience? Is there a deeper under-standing of their reference to a kingdom of peace with justice, one that relates to today's reality and not simply to a personal eschatological/future hope?

2   Remembering personal stories is integral to maintaining and sustaining a sense of identity. Take time to reflect on your own sense of identity: on what, with whom is it based? Jesus calls his followers to be peacemakers. How fully is that integrated into who you are? Is the demand too great?

3   Being alongside the Sea of Galilee is a sharp reminder of the importance of water in everyday life. A closer look today will show clear signs of the water level being depleted. The misuse and abuse of water is common throughout the developing world. Jesus' claim to be the 'living water' (John 4.10) is not only a spiritual quenching but one requiring humanitarian action of his followers. Are there ways in which you continue to nourish yourself, mindful of the imperative of providing equal access to others?

4 Spend some time, with others if possible, reflecting on your use and understanding of 'shalom'. Has the word tripped off your tongue as an easy greeting or happy 'farewell'? A comprehensive understanding includes its moral character, which demands of its users the integration of word with *actions*. Will this help or hinder your use of 'shalom' in future?

2

Desert experience and the time of testing and trial

———•◦•———

> The desert waits,
> ready for those who come,
> who come obedient to the Spirit's leading;
> or who are driven,
> because they will not come any other way.
>
> The desert always waits,
> ready to let us know who we are –
> the place of self-discovery.
>
> And whilst we fear, and rightly,
> the loneliness and emptiness and harshness,
> we forget the angels,
> whom we cannot see for our blindness,
> but who come when God decides
> that we need their help;
> when we are ready
> for what they can give us.   Ruth Burgess[1]

Deserts evoke polarized reactions: as I write,[2] the world is haunted by the tragedy of thousands of hunger-stricken women, men and children fleeing the drought and famine of desert regions of Ethiopia, Somalia and Kenya to the largest refugee camp in the world at Dabaab, Northern Kenya. Deserts are often places of suffering, where people, animals and plants alike struggle to survive at the very edge of their limits of endurance; where the land itself manifests the consequences of the harsh climate and years of mismanagement and degradation. Politics, ecology and economics all play a role. Yet at the same time deserts, as the poem above acknowledges, have a long history in

Christian spirituality and Judaism as places for solitude, reflection, commissioning and inspiration. This double-sidedness is vital for the movement of this chapter. The desert experience for Jesus, as time of temptation, trial and testing, is the frame for the challenge that faces Christians today on our own Lenten pilgrimage, not only personally but for the wider issues of structural violence that block the possibility of the realization of the kingdom of God.

The desert – spiritual and physical

Whereas Galilee set the scene for Jesus' ministry (see Chapter 1), the Temptation stories take us to places both geographical, political and metaphorical.[3] In a sense it does not matter *where* the Temptations actually happened – except, of course, for the people who live in deserts today and struggle to eke out a living in the very places Jesus spent '40 days'. Many sites claim to be the place of the Temptations – especially since Matthew and Luke imply considerable movement, from the wilderness to a mountain and to the Jerusalem Temple itself (in different sequences). This example is only one possibility of locating a site. Also in Jerusalem, on the Temple Mount, is a Byzantine shrine, the Church of the Pinnacle, marking one of the presumed sites of Jesus' Temptations.

The Monastery of Temptation, Jericho

About 3 kilometres north-west of Jericho, the summit of the Mount of Temptation, rising to 350 metres above sea level, commands a magnificent and panoramic view of the Jordan Valley: this is the presumed site where Jesus spent 40 days and 40 nights fasting and meditating during the temptation of Satan. When visiting this in January 2012 I was totally unprepared for the grimness and isolation of this rocky scene in the Judean desert.

A Greek Orthodox monastery was built in the sixth century over the cave where Christ is thought to have stayed. This is another of the holy sites said to have been identified by the Empress Helena in her pilgrimage of 326 CE. The mountain that from early Christian times has been called the Mount of Temptation was referred to as *Mons Quarantana* by the Crusaders in the first half of the twelfth century, and is locally known as Quruntul mountain (from Quaranta meaning 40, the number of days in the Gospel account of Christ's stay in the desert). To climb up the bare, rocky slopes of Quruntul mountain would be daunting indeed, as the path leading to the Monastery is very steep: the pilgrim today is offered the choice of the cable car! Even so the walk at the top is steep. The sides of the mountain are dotted with caves, some marked by crosses. Nearly 30 to 40 caves on the eastern slopes of the mountain have been inhabited by monks and hermits since the early days of Christianity.

But the meaning of the Gospel story lies at a deeper level than identifying a site! Indeed, the Synoptics all carry a clear message. After his baptism in the Jordan, Jesus was 'driven' ('hurled' – as Mark says[4]), 'led' (Matthew and Luke), into the desert – *eremos* (wilderness or lonely place). In each case the Holy Spirit took the initiative. *Eremos*[5] has a special significance for Mark. As Ched Myers tells us, it is a crucial coordinate for his narrative:

> In literal terms, wilderness connoted an uninhabited and desolate place, marginal existence: John lives on locusts and honey, and persons hunger there. Symbolically it was the site of a community in flight (as in the exodus tradition) or a refuge for the persecuted faithful who await deliverance . . . Jesus, like Israel, is 'tested' there; there he seeks solitude. In this, both Jesus and John follow the prophetic script of Elijah, who also withdrew to the wilderness, when hunted by the political authorities (1 Kings 19).[6]

In addition to the Exodus and Elijah background, I add Moses' wilderness experience as he encountered God in the burning bush on Mount Horeb.[7] The wilderness is also the place from which prophetic and revolutionary movements sprang. It is thought that Jesus – and John the Baptist – may have spent time with the Essene community in the desert. The Synoptics present it to us as the symbolic space of repentance, contrasted with Jerusalem, where unjust power systems – both religious and political – still held sway.

In contemporary Israel, both the Judean and Negev deserts help us to re-imagine the wilderness/*eremos* context in Jesus' time, even though a landscape is never static as it undergoes continual changes and adaptations to climate. The Negev is no exception: since early Christianity it flourished as a place of the founding of many monasteries – especially that of St Catherine on Mount Sinai. Pilgrimages brought income to towns in the Negev – indeed, its freshly grown fruit and vegetables delivered income to the Empire.[8] After Islam swept through the Negev in the seventh century in its conquest of Palestine, the inhabitants of the region slowly left their homes. A nineteenth-century traveller described its isolation and abandonment: 'There stood the ancient towns, still called by their ancient names, but not a living thing was to be seen, save when a lizard glided over the crumbling walls, or screech owls flitted through the lonely streets.'[9]

This happened because the Islamic rulers had little use for the desert – the borders of their empire that needed guarding by military outposts lay far to the west. So the Negev was left as home to Bedouin nomads for hundreds of years: many eked out a living at subsistence level, although recent scholarship shows their culture as far more complex and sophisticated than once assumed. In any case things were to change after the founding of the state of Israel in 1948.[10]

What, then, were the wilderness conditions for Jesus? Mark alone tells us that 'he was with the wild beasts'.[11] This detail, which for the Gospel writer had apocalyptic significance, allows us to imagine the camels, sheep, goats and donkeys that were traditional domestic animals for desert dwellers as well as gazelle, ibex and other forms of deer. Wild animals adapt well to severe climatic conditions – I have seen small wiry deer in the desert of Rajasthan that are almost indistinguishable from the sand dunes and sparse vegetation. There would also have been wild animals (the real meaning of *theria*, Mark's word), such as hyena, the desert fox (Jesus' name for Herod Antipas), the lynx, wild cat, snakes, scorpions and many rodents and insects – all of which survive well in drought conditions. Animal symbolism seen apocalyptically is assumed to point to the beasts in Daniel 7.3, and Revelation 11.7 with political reference to the powers of oppression and domination. I think Isaiah 11 also lies behind this text: that if, in messianic times, 'the wolf shall lie down with the lamb, the leopard shall lie down with the kid' (Isaiah 11.6) in a context of peace with human beings and the whole of nature, this is what Jesus' proclamation of the kingdom will bring about. So what are the writers telling us about the real meaning of temptation for Jesus?

The time of testing and trial

Mark sets a brief but dramatic, apocalyptic contest between Jesus and Satan, with the angels at hand to minister to him just as they did to Elijah in the wilderness.[12] (It is interesting that Luke, given the role that angels played in his Gospel, omits the detail about the angels' ministry.)

For Satan we should also understand the entire first-century world of demons. The casting out of demons is integral to the healing ministry and proclamation of the kingdom in all Synoptic Gospels – we should resist today's rationalizing tendency to overlook its significance. Initially it might seem that this world-view has no connection with the rational empiricism of contemporary life. Yet there are many links with modern Palestine, as the ethnographer and medical pioneer Tawfiq Canaan shows. He believed that the peasants of Palestine represent – through their folk norms – the living heritage of all the accumulated ancient cultures that had appeared in Palestine (principally the Canaanite, Philistine, Hebraic, Nabatean, Syrio-Aramaic and Arab). In his book, *Belief in Demons in the Holy Land*,[13] Canaan gathered together every reference to demons in Palestinian popular belief, detailing their names and classes, food, dress, appearance and dwellings, for example the carob tree. Canaan considered that village sanctuaries and rituals confer protection and blessings, and these were an indication of how supernatural forces are found everywhere, affecting people's lives, bringing good or bad luck and even diseases. The names of some diseases in Arabic reference the names of long-forgotten demons, such as *al-khanuq* (diphtheria), *ar-rih al-asfar* (cholera or yellow fever) and *at-ta'un* (plague). Canaan's perception of the origin of demons was in line with the traditional view that they were once deities within the polytheistic system – what Canaan refers to as 'primitive religions'. With the advent of monotheism, the status of these gods diminished, subsisting nevertheless in the community unconscious as demons.

Demons (or jinns) especially haunted lonely places, caves, cracks in the earth where the sun could not reach. Today garbage dumps and bathrooms are places where, it is believed, jinns still manifest themselves. Historically speaking, springs and cisterns were especially chosen, wrote Canaan in his famous paper, *Haunted Springs and Water Demons in Palestine*.[14] Jinns are still very much part of local culture in contemporary Palestine. Celia E. Rothenberg, in *Spirits of Palestine*, writes of the complexities of the phenomena, following her research in Artas, a village near Bethlehem.[15] Most of her examples are Muslim stories, the jinn being thought of as a Muslim spirit, though one person she describes has a Christian background. It is too simplistic to dismiss the cultural experience of possession by the jinn – often described as 'wearing the jinn' – as mental illness as such, although some of the expressions, such as screams and convulsions, look identical to some expressions of mental illnesses. Rather, they could be seen as offering strategies for coping with current difficulties and even suffering, through traditional cultural phenomena. Palestinian Muslim society makes subtle distinctions between mental illness, sickness and spirit possession. In some of the cases described, women appear to be rebuked because they are 'unclean' or do not pray the Qur'an enough. (The burden of 'women's work' that allows men to pray but gives no time to women is a frequent complaint.) Many stories relate to infertility and arranged marriages.

I cite these contemporary examples because they also give a window into the world of Jesus and his struggle with demons as presented by the Synoptic Gospels. These comparisons also point to the complexity of transformation necessary from being dominated by evil spirits to the new way offered by Jesus.[16]

The wilderness contest is between the demons of destruction and the Spirit of peace and justice. Though Mark gives us no details as to the nature of the Temptations, by preceding the passage with the quotation from the prophet Malachi ('See, I am sending my messenger ahead of you') and from Isaiah ('a voice cries out in the wilderness'), both referring to John the Baptist, together with the revelation of Jesus at his baptism as 'my Son, the Beloved',[17] Mark proclaims a profound message that will permeate his entire story – political yet transcending the politics of the day. Two powerful Old Testament themes of salvation are united in the person of Jesus – the divine warrior motif and the return from exile. As Willard Swartley tells us: 'In these Exodus and Isaiahan texts the divine warfare of the conquest is fused with the festal procession of Israel's trek through the desert/wilderness returning home from exile.'[18]

And the political message is that the current system of power and social organization is not only deficient and corrupt, but evil: the prevailing order will be replaced by a new order of peace and justice. Jesus will overturn the warrior motif: his leadership is one of shepherding, of love and care. It is not merely that the cruel domination of the Roman Empire will be overturned, that violence will be transformed by non-violence, but that a kingdom of a totally different kind will be ushered in. The warrior hero will be replaced by re-imaging the very notion of hero into a figure of peace and non-violence.[19]

Luke and Matthew both depict Jesus as tempted by Empire models of power: almost starving, he is taunted to turn stones into bread; to test the power of God by hurling himself from the Temple pinnacle; and to gain all the kingdoms of the world if he would worship Satan.[20] At a distance it is easy for us to underestimate how serious is the time of testing for Jesus. His whole destiny and mission are at stake. His baptism revealed the initial profundity of the task: after being named as 'my Son, the Beloved', in Mark's urgent account Jesus is literally propelled into the wilderness, at the same time 'full of the Spirit', as Luke says. We can see how seriously Jesus understood this 'time of trial' (*peirasmos*) because the theme recurs. It appears again as part of the 'Our Father' (in Matthew this is included in the Sermon on the Mount): 'And do not bring us to the time of trial'.[21] In Luke it appears slightly later, in exactly the same form, when the disciples, seeing Jesus at prayer, ask him to teach them to pray.[22] But even more dramatically, the phrase reappears at Jesus' time of greatest trial, on the Mount of Olives, before his arrest, when he prayed to God that the cup of suffering be removed from him. Yet 'not my will but yours be done'.[23] Poignantly, it is the time when the chosen apostles were asked to stay awake and watch one hour with him, yet slept: 'Get up and pray that you may not come into the time of trial [*peirasmos*]', he says sadly. Has he been living with this *peirasmos* from this time in the wilderness? And what does it mean?

It means that Jesus, inspired by the Spirit and in communion with God, enters into an understanding of a vision of the kingdom and his unique responsibility in its proclamation – unique because his self-understanding within his relationship with God is unfolding dramatically. Without question, it was a vision that opposed the violence of the Roman domination. To read any text of the Roman Empire is to be appalled by the extent of brutal killing that was the norm, from the emperors downwards – even with regard to their own families, wives and children.[24] Even if we assume that our modern society is more 'civilized', we only need to think of instances of torture in which we are involved (such as instances of 'extraordinary rendition),[25] of the killing of civilians in Afghanistan, as well as political systems legitimizing violence and killing in different parts of the world with whom we are allied, or give support to, openly or behind the scenes. Civilian deaths are steadily increasing.

Yet we know that Jesus distanced himself from the Zealots and the movements to expel the Romans violently. The ethos of the kingdom would embody a different kind of kingship: a sense of humility and meekness would characterize it – 'Blessed are the meek' as the Sermon on the Mount proclaimed.[26] Meekness, gentleness and humility are offered by a king who entered Jerusalem on a donkey[27] and whose yoke – as opposed to the yoke of the Romans – was light.[28]

At the Sabeel conference in Bethlehem in March 2011, 'Challenging Empire: God, Faithfulness and Resistance', the sermon inaugurating the conference, entitled 'Blessed are the Meek', was preached by the Lutheran Church Pastor of Bethlehem, Mitri Raheb, at the Wi'am Reconciliation Centre, with the Israeli 'Security Wall' behind him and Aida Refugee Camp on his right. His message was dramatic: the Greek and Roman Empires have been and gone; similarly the Ottoman, British and Jordanian – so the meek will inherit because they are the only ones left behind!

But Jesus meant more: 'meek' does not mean being passive or not resisting injustice. Like John Howard Yoder, I believe Jesus' message was socially, politically and economically revolutionary, and that he took radical stances against practices of oppression and accumulation of riches.[29] But he also addressed the stark fact that often the revolution may be won but people may not have been healed. Unless the Christic vision can set in motion processes of reconciliation that release the forces of evil from the depths of the heart of all conflicting parties, especially intergenerationally, peace with justice always eludes realization.

This is the central point about the Temptation, the stomach-churning challenge, the cup that was too painful to drink. We miss the depth of its demands if we remain only at the level of Jesus' wanderings around Galilee, healing and exorcising: these were indeed an integral part of achieving the goal – that people be liberated from every kind of blockage, be these hunger, sickness, poverty, demonic possession – to enable healing and transformation. It was a healing that opened out to Gentiles – as witnessed by the healing of the Roman centurion's paralysed servant.[30] But these were part of the profounder commitment, the replacement of structures of domination and value systems of Empire that justified all kinds of evil, and considered as valueless all vulnerable categories of people. Rather, vulnerable people are to be at the centre of God's project. Children, women without respect and legal rights, slaves and despised categories (such as the former Untouchables in India, today's Dalits) are to attain honoured places in the emerging community where the ethic of forgiveness will hold pride of place. No racism, no gender hierarchies: the goal was the destabilization of hierarchy itself.

But what a commitment this demanded and what a price to be paid, as any disciple of non-violence throughout the ages has realized. Small wonder that Martin Scorsese in his controversial film *The Last Temptation* showed the dying Jesus on the cross, tempted to give in and opt for a life of happiness with Mary Magdalen.[31] 'What about the kingdom?' cry his shocked disciples, back from the mission. With his last breath Jesus recommits to the dream, and dies. Jesus, Gandhi, Martin Luther King and today the Burmese politician Aung San Suu Kyi, all witness to the freely chosen path of suffering and sacrifice for the achievement of radical freedom for their people. In her recent Reith Lecture, Aung San Suu Kyi – freed from her 19 years of house arrest – movingly described the vocation of who, non-violently, resist oppression for the sake of justice as one of *passion*, a passion for liberty, but playing on the double meaning of the word:

> Passion translates as suffering and I would contend that in the political context, as in the religious one, it implies suffering by choice: a deliberate decision to grasp the cup that we would rather let pass. It is not a decision made lightly – we do not enjoy suffering; we are not masochists. It is because of the high value we put on the object of our passion that we are able, sometimes in spite of ourselves, to choose suffering.[32]

Passion is for liberty, and, yes, she emphasizes spiritual freedom as vital – but that is not the total picture. Fear is never far away – and this must have been an ever present reality to Jesus:

> Fear is the first adversary we have to get past when we set out to battle for freedom, and often it is the one that remains until the very end. But freedom from fear does not have to be complete. It only has to be sufficient to enable us to carry on; and to carry on in spite of fear requires tremendous courage.
>
> *'No, I am not afraid. After a year of breathing these prison nights, I will escape into the sadness to name which is escape. It isn't true. I am afraid, my darling, but make it look as though you haven't noticed.'*
>
> The gallantry embodied in Ratushinskaya's lines is everyday fare for dissidents. They pretend to be unafraid as they go about their duties and pretend not to see that their comrades are also pretending. This is not hypocrisy. This is courage that has to be renewed consciously from day to day and moment to moment. This is how the battle for freedom has to be fought until such time as we have the right to be free from the fear imposed by brutality and injustice.[33]

Her words bring alive for us what was at stake for Jesus in that crucial time of testing. Not only fear of violence on the part of the authorities but the real fear that he would be misunderstood not only by his closest followers but by his own family. Yet Jesus did emerge from the time and place of trial, energized – thanks to the angels – to begin proclaiming the coming kingdom.

Contemporary pilgrimage and our time of testing

As Jesus was, we too are 'hurled' into the Desert. And first we need to confront the struggle for survival of the desert peoples of the world today, in a context of worsening drought due to climate change, specifically here the Bedouin of Israel/Palestine.

The distinction between Bedouin and non-Bedouin communities is mainly an anthropological one, but there is an important difference: Bedouin communities have a tribally based socio-cultural system and a semi-nomadic way of life, whereas non-Bedouin herding communities are traditionally linked to Palestinian villages. Following the 1948 conflict, Bedouin communities were obliged to abandon their traditional lands in the Negev to splinter into smaller social units and disperse as refugees, diluting tribal leadership structures and socio-cultural traditions.[34]

So who are the Bedouin?

> With their camels, flowing robes and warm hospitality, the Bedouin have long been the symbol of life in the harsh desert, brought to fame as the desert warriors who guided Lawrence of Arabia during his First World War campaign against the Ottomans in the Middle East. Many can still pull out land deeds dating to the Ottoman Empire or at least the more recent British mandate, establishing their traditional territory, and historians say evidence of their existence here stretches back beyond the eleventh century BCE.[35]

The Bedouin of the Negev are traditionally pastoral semi-nomadic Arab tribes indigenous to the Negev region in Israel, holding close ties to the Bedouin of the Sinai Peninsula. Many Bedouin have been urbanized, promised services in exchange for the renunciation of their ancestral land. Denied access to their former sources of sustenance via grazing restrictions, severed from the possibility of access to water, electricity, roads, education and health care in villages unrecognized by the government, the plight of the Bedouin today is extremely grave.[36] Some Negev Bedouin still have goats and sheep. Pilgrims to Israel will observe Bedouin settlements – poor tin shacks by roadsides – and will be hassled by men with donkeys desperate to sell necklaces and scarves to tourists, simply to have food to eat.

Such is the current state of the once proud desert dwellers whose struggle for justice lays claim on our compassion and responsibility. As many of their problems cluster around access to water, and water is a prominent theme in the struggle for justice in all drought-prone areas, this chapter ends by highlighting this issue in Israel/Palestine.

Water scientists focus on Middle Eastern water needs as a whole. In the Levant, water is the most important guarantor of a state's sovereignty, allowing it to direct development and provide food security independently for its people. It is possible that climate change may even bring benefits to the region if, for example, seasonal flooding in the Nile basin can be channelled elsewhere to needy regions; if salinity problems and the treatment of sewage can be looked at on a regional and not just a nationalistic basis. But at the moment the urgency is focused on just access to water for Bedouin and Palestinians as a whole. As Wilson Dizard writes:

> For the last six decades, Palestinians have been trying to carve a new country from a rapidly evaporating pool of liquid sovereignty. Unfortunately for Palestinian aspirations for statehood, every groundwater resource in the West Bank and Gaza Strip sits beneath its borders with Israel. While Oslo II in 1995 laid out allocations from the shared aquifers, the divisions have grown obsolete after 14 years of population growth. And while Israel uses the martial mechanisms of occupation to restrict Palestinian access to aquifers, it routinely flouts the limits Oslo set.[37]

According to many sources, including the World Bank, in some parts of the West Bank, like the suburbs of Hebron, Palestinian villagers and semi-nomadic Bedouin far from water infrastructure have to manage to survive on as little as 15 litres of water a day, often bought at exorbitant prices from roving water tankers. (This is the same predicament for many drought-stricken areas of the world: water is the new gold in these stressed places.) In addition, Israel dumps waste water and solid waste on land above Palestinian villages and has moved polluting industries to the West Bank as well as industrial waste.[38] These bare facts are reinforced by many personal stories of hardship, as any visitor to the region will testify. Wilson Dizard concludes:

> Israel has its back up against a security fence when it comes to water. Since its independence, Israel has made exceptional efforts to control the region's water resources, at first necessary for the cultivation of national pride and identity through agriculture. Farming still takes the lion's share of Israel's water supplies. With economic development,

population growth, and an immigration policy designed to replace Palestinian labourers with foreign hands, Israel's demand for water has risen, straining the ecological balance between human beings and their environment.[39]

If we follow Jesus' redemptive way, reflecting on the meaning of the desert experience for the pilgrim people of today, these are precisely the kind of justice issues to be confronted. They lie at a deeper level than the simple challenge – 'Shall we give up chocolate and alcohol for Lent?' – and demand that justice for both earth and people be factored in to any understanding of redemption. A different kind of asceticism is called for. As this chapter has shown, the level of commitment to the kingdom proclaimed by Jesus will cost nothing less than a lifetime of costly discipleship. Is our temptation, or 'time of trial' (*peirasmos*), to refuse to face the truth once we have become aware of it, to turn away from the complexity of the Arab/Israeli conflict and to betray the appeal made to us by Jesus' covenant of peace, a peace that wanted to enfold all nations in his time and in our own?

Questions for reflection

1 Making a retreat is often viewed as a desert or wilderness experience. Those on retreat often describe this as 'facing my demons' which, when faced, ultimately lead to the inner cleansing implicit in coming closer to God. Does this resonate with any similar moments on your own journey of faith? Give thanks to God for all you have learnt through them.

2 If you found yourself uncomfortable with the concept of 'demons', you might like to reflect on the attraction in today's media culture of vampires and witches (and *Harry Potter*). What might this be saying to today's understanding of 'good' and 'evil', and how it is expressed?

3 The most frequent reminder of Jesus' testing in the wilderness is in praying the Lord's Prayer. Routinely we pray 'Lead us not into *temptation*', yet if taken from recent translations of the New Testament, a more accurate phrase would be, as I have used above, 'And do not bring us to the *time of trial*' (Matthew 6.9;

Luke 11.4 – see also Mark 13.11; Luke 22.40: in the Garden of Gethsemane). What difference would this change of wording make to you? There is an implied shift from a personal and private challenge to a public indictment: how might this affect your perception of discipleship? You might like to ask yourself, 'If brought to trial as a disciple of Jesus, would there be enough evidence to convict me?'

4 Having faced the challenges of the wilderness, Jesus engages with the reality of what is to be his ministry, placing 'vulnerable people' at the centre. Who would you identify as being 'vulnerable' within today's society? Are you able to recognize them as people for whom you have a direct responsibility? Take time to reflect on how you understand the value of each human being. How might this impact on your ministry of reconciliation?

3

The Mount of Transfiguration

> We'll just say that we've been to the mountain
> and caught a glimpse of all that we could be;
> we will know that a new day is dawning,
> with a morning sun for all of us to see.
> > Tim McAllister[1]

These moments are given to us so that we can remember them when God seems far away and everything seems empty and useless. These experiences are true moments of grace.   Henry Nouwen[2]

The Transfiguration represents a turning point. From this moment Jesus sets his face toward Jerusalem.   Andrew Ashdown[3]

The Lenten journey now takes an unexpected turn – to climb up the high Mount of Transfiguration with Jesus and his three chosen disciples, Peter, James and John.[4] Traditionally, since the Transfiguration has its own feast day on 6 August,[5] its place here is normally explained as a break from the Lenten routine, and a foretaste of Easter glory. This chapter explores a deeper meaning, since Jesus' transfiguration is interpreted here through the chosen lens of enduring conflict and Palestinian suffering.

Which mountain?

Two sites are usually considered as the place of the Mount of Transfiguration. The most popular has been Mount Tabor, which is at the eastern end of the Jezreel valley, about 18 kilometres south-west of the Sea of Galilee.[6] Almost 600 metres high, it is seen in the Bible as a symbol of majesty[7] as well as being the site of Deborah's battle, where Barak led the Israelite charge of 10,000 men against Sisera and the Canaanite army.[8] Early Church fathers, including Cyril of Jerusalem (in 348 CE), Epiphanius and St Jerome, believed that the Transfiguration took place on Mount Tabor. Eastern theologians like St Gregory Nazianzen and St John of Damascus focus less on the location and more on the revelation of divine splendour to the apostles. The historian Eusebius was uncertain if this revelation took place on Mount Tabor or on Mount Hermon – the other candidate. Israeli Palestinian Muslim historian Nur Masalha, whose ancestral village, Daburiyya, like Mount Tabor, lies in lower Galilee, between the mountains of Nazareth and Mount Tabor, tells of the popularity of Mount Tabor as a pilgrimage site:

> Of course Mount Tabor (we call it *Jabal al-Tur*) is famous because the site is connected to the Christian tradition of Transfiguration (the 'Mount of Transfiguration') ... every year hundreds of people from Nazareth and Palestinian Christians from the Galilee arrive and camp for days at the site during the feast of Transfiguration.[9]

Many of Professor Masalha's relatives have houses on the lower slopes of the mountain. He recalls, when he was a child, the hundreds of coaches full of European and American pilgrims and tourists arriving every year, parking at one end of the village then being taken by taxis to the summit of the mountain. Historically and strategically, he continues, the mountain dominated the whole area and must have been a holy site since antiquity. Many rulers, including the Crusaders and later Saladin, built fortresses at the summit – Byzantine, Crusader and Muslim:

> [W]hen I was a child we used to go up to the summit very often ... sometimes to pick up mushrooms ... a few times, too, as school kids and scouts ... but often just to look at the spectacular surrounding scenery ... you can see for miles in all directions.[10]

The people of this Muslim village, Daburiyya, were always on good terms with the monks living at the summit of the mountain – some of the villagers even worked for them.

One reason for the confusion between the two sites was a misunderstanding of Matthew 17.1. This verse was taken to mean that Jesus took the disciples up a mountain 'by itself',[11] rather than that he took the disciples up a mountain 'by themselves'. Also, Mount Tabor has been questioned as being too far away from the Sea of Galilee to fit the biblical story. But the main problem, wrote Bargil Pixner, was that Mount Tabor at the time was populated and, as Nur Masalha's memories indicate, a Hasmonean fortress would have stood on its summit.[12] How could Jesus have chosen solitude there? There is also a long tradition associated with Mount Hermon, rising high in the Golan Heights and covered in snow for most of the year: it is considered locally as a holy mountain.

Yet as with the previous chapter's discussion as to where the Mount of Temptation was located, the focus here is more on the meaning of the story for the Lenten quest than establishing definitively its geographical site. Despite the issue of historical veracity, the continuing popularity of the Basilica of the Transfiguration on Mount Tabor as place of pilgrimage will always be important.[13]

We'll just say that we've been to the mountain

Our question must be: What does this experience say to us in the context of the Lenten pilgrimage and of the yearning for justice in the Bible lands? It is becoming more popular in Christian spirituality to give the Transfiguration a wider spiritual meaning, namely, as the opening Henri Nouwen and Tim McAllister quotations indicate, as a reference not only to a dominating peak experience but to moments of transcendence and glory that offer a transfiguring quality for the entirety of life. As Robert Browning expressed it:

> Just as we are safest, there's a sunset touch,
> a fancy from a flowerbell, some one's death,
> a chorus ending from Euripides, –
> and that's enough for fifty hopes and fears.[14]

In 1974 the American writer Annie Dillard evoked the abiding glow of this enduring transfiguring experience in her vision of the 'Tree with Lights':

I saw the backyard cedar where the mourning doves roost charged and transfigured, each cell buzzing with flame. I stood on the grass with the lights in it, grass that was wholly fire, utterly focused and utterly dreamed. It was less like seeing than like being for the first time seen, knocked breathless by a powerful glance. The flood of fire abated, but I'm still spending the power . . . The vision comes and goes, mostly goes, but I live for it, for the moment when the mountains open and a new light roars in spate through the crack, and the mountains slam.[15]

Divine light, or *la lumière taborique*, is the way Eastern Orthodox theology characterizes the Transfiguration.[16] Annie Dillard's powerful passage evokes the transfiguring, enduring nature of the experience for a lifetime, but *nothing* of the context of the Gospel account. We cannot ignore the fact that the evangelists tell us of the danger that frames this experience. Early in Luke's chapter, Herod is asking who Jesus was: hadn't he, Herod, just beheaded John to be rid of trouble-makers (9.9)? Jesus has fed the multitude but the day ends with his telling the disciples that 'The Son of Man must undergo great suffering' (9.21). Eight days later – Luke is exact – comes the mountain journey, and the chapter ends with the Gospel's great turning point: 'When the days drew near for him to be taken up, he set his face to go to Jerusalem' (9.51).

This is the frame for the mountain experience. A recent social-scientific approach to the story interprets it against the Near Eastern/ Mediterranean culture of a densely populated spirit world and the trance-like, waking dream phenomenon that forms part of this, enabling communication with angelic or demonic spirits.[17] According to this interpretation, Jesus entered this trance-like state ('alternative state of consciousness' or ASC), needing to acquire more depth of understanding about his mission and ministry. His focus is his personal communication with God; the disciples' focus is Jesus – and the two 'men', whom they identify as Moses and Elijah. The radiant brightness is sometimes likened to the contemporary experience of someone's 'aura'.[18] It can be compared with the state of enlightenment of Buddhism or moments of radiant enlightenment sometimes referred to as 'Buddha moments'.

Comparison is sometimes made with the story of Muhammad's night-time journey (or *Al-Isra wa Al-Miraj*), *c.* 619 CE, which can be given a historical, psychological or mystical explanation. After the appearance of the angel Gabriel, Muhammad, at a significant juncture in his life, was taken by a winged horse, *al Buraq*, high into the heavens, and then to the 'Furthest Mosque' in Jerusalem.[19] Here he leads other prophets including Adem (Adam), Musa (Moses) and Isa (Jesus) in prayer. In the second part of the journey, he is taken to the seven heavens, where he speaks with prophets such as Abraham and again Moses and Jesus. He is then taken by the angel to meet God. The spiritual impact of this journey is more crucial than its historicity.[20] Muhammad, like Jesus on the mountain, at a significant moment in his life, converses with prophets in a mystical journey that actually takes him to the highest heavens, into the presence of God.

What is remarkable about Luke's story, in comparison with the other two Gospel writers, is his more subdued tone: Jesus' face did not shine like the sun (Matthew), and even though his clothing became as 'brilliant as lightning', Luke does not use Mark's rapturous description. Neither Matthew nor Mark refers to the content of the conversation with Moses and Elijah, but Luke tells us that they discussed the 'exodus' that Jesus was about to fulfil in Jerusalem. How significant that Moses, prophet, leader of the Israelite exodus from Egypt and receiver of the covenant on Mount Sinai, and Elijah, who had experienced his own exodus and divine revelation on Mount Horeb,[21] should be in conversation with the Beloved Son, about to set his face to Jerusalem – and thereby setting *all* peoples free.

So we should see this experience as pointing forward to the dénouement in the Holy City. The mistake the disciples make is to assume the eschatological moment has come and to prolong the experience by wanting to build shrines. As Paul Evdokimov explained:

> In the Gospel story, the focus is on Christ Transfigured. But the Transfiguration is in fact that of the apostles, who, for a moment, pass 'from flesh to spirit', and receive the grace of seeing the humanity of Christ as a body transfigured with light, of contemplating the glory of the Lord hidden under his *kenosis*,[22] and abruptly unveiled before their astonished eyes. This light is the energy through which God offers Godself entirely and the vision constitutes the 'face-to-face', the mystery of the Eighth Day, and the state of deification.[23]

But not yet. The journey still had to be undergone, then and now. Perhaps the apostles were wrong in clinging to the moment: in hindsight we as readers know they are to betray, desert, yet be reunited with Jesus, post-resurrection. Yet in and through these terrible experiences they had been given a vision and they would not forget it. As Peter tells us later: '"This is my Son, my Beloved, with whom I am well pleased." We ourselves heard this voice come from heaven, while we were with him on the holy mountain.'[24]

Being given a vision is one thing, but how do we know that the transfiguring experience, the lightning moment of glory prefiguring the fullness of time (or eschaton), is offered to all humanity? I return to the introduction of this book, where I appealed to us to become aware of the lens through which we read the Scriptures. Nowhere is this more crucial than the way in which we understand creation stories, especially Genesis 1 and 2. If we understand them literally as God creating the cosmos in seven days (including a day of rest), not only do we fall into the literalist trap, with a trail of consequences, but we miss the rich theological depth offered by the stories.

The theologian Neil Douglas-Klotz explains the complexity of the origins of the many creation stories (including those found in Isaiah, the Proverbs and Job), and offers an illuminating idea that Hebrew mystics worked with creation stories as *spiritual practices*:

> In the ancient worldview inherent in Semitic languages, time does not exist like a line extending from past to future with ourselves existing outside it at one particular point on the line and no other. Instead, the ancient Hebrews saw their beginnings moving ahead of them carrying them along, with their future following behind, also moving at the same time. One could in this sense feel both the past and future actively part of one's life and, in a state of intense meditation, unite all moments in one.[25]

This is not so alien to ordinary Christian practice: what else does the prayer 'Glory be to the Father' imply when we pray 'as it was in the beginning, is now and ever shall be' but the belief that the power of the creation can be brought into the present? Meditating in this way means attempting to experience a connection to the life and sacred power of the creation moment and what it means to be in the divine image. This is what John is trying to convey in his Prologue: 'In the beginning was the word . . . And the word became flesh and lived among us.'[26]

It is also the meaning of the Transfiguration for us today – 'the Message and Conversation that has not stopped and has never started because it is always Now'.[27] Neil Douglas-Klotz gives us a beautiful rendering of this meaning:

> You are now experiencing in yourselves, my Beloved, the child of the Cosmos, the one who brings into the world love to give, love to receive. Through this radiant reflection, the image of your original Self, I express the joy of the Universe, the passion and desire that holds everything together. Don't hold on. Why not just listen? Open your ears to the universal sound![28]

As David Adam of the Northumbrian community wrote: 'Here is a vision of humankind as it could be; how through fulfilling the law and the prophets, each of us can reveal and share in the glory of God.'[29]

Was the Trappist monk Thomas Merton convinced of this as, in his vision experience in Louisville, Kentucky, he cried out, 'How do you tell people they are all walking around shining like the sun?!'[30] But how can this radiance, this offered transfiguration, and return to the 'original Self' of creation, become earthed in a context of suffering and, frequently, loss of hope? As Tim McAllister's hymn, a quotation from which also started this chapter, cries out:

> In the rays of the sunrise, we find the warmth of new life.
> Our faith is strengthened as the mysteries unfold;
> where lies the answer?
> How will we know?[31]

The transfiguring vision and Palestinian sumud

There is no easy answer to the question McAllister's hymn asks. It is possible that the lack of an easy answer is what drove Jesus up the mountain to seek divine light in the first place. But Palestinian Christian faith is built on sturdy roots, deep in the very soil to which they so passionately cling. There is already a sustaining vision, nurtured by centuries of belonging to this land, by the beauty of cultural memories, ancient Christian feasts celebrated with pride, and by the aesthetic traditions of poetry, art, drama, social theatre and dance. And there is the spirituality of *sumud*, steadfastness, persistence and patient endurance.[32] It could have been for contemporary Palestinians that the prophet Habakkuk (probably active around 615 BCE) wrote these words in response to God's command:

> Write the vision;
>   make it plain on the tablets ...
> For there is still a vision for the appointed time;
>   it speaks of the end, and does not lie.
> If it seems to tarry, wait for it;
>   it will surely come, it will not delay![33]

It is interesting that an eighteenth-century Russian icon of the prophet Habakkuk is found on the Iconostasis[34] of the Transfiguration Church, in the Kizhi monastery of Karelia in Russia: it is as if Habakkuk's vision refers to the enduring quality of the Transfiguration. Is *sumud* a way of holding on to the vision?

It was *sumud* when Aung San Suu Kyi endured house arrest but refused to surrender the vision of freedom and justice for her people; it was *sumud* when Nelson Mandela emerged from 27 years of imprisonment on Robben Island and refused to give way to violent revenge on his captors, but lived from a purified vision of non-violent reconciliation.[35]

Toine van Teeffelen and Fuad Giacaman of the Arab Education Institute in Bethlehem are continually evolving new expressions of *sumud*.[36] Van Teeffelen defined the *sumud* concept as, on the one hand, relating 'to a vertical dimension of Palestinian life, "standing strong" on the land, having deep roots'. On the other hand, *sumud* 'indicates a horizontal time dimension – an attitude of patience and persistence, of not giving up, despite the odds'.[37] Motivated by the need to find sources of hope in the present context, the Arab Educational Institute in recent years has developed pedagogical applications of the *sumud* concept, taking it outside strictly political boundaries. The following values are stressed as constitutive of *sumud*: its democratic or participative character, openness to many different life stories, agency or willpower, an aesthetic perspective and the possibility of connecting *sumud* with wider human values and circles of community.

A striking interpretation of *sumud* has been offered by the lawyer Raja Shehadeh, who sees it as a non-violent attitude of life that could forge a third way between acceptance of the occupation and opting for violent struggle: through this he gave a voice to many Palestinians who refused to leave their land and tried to go on with their daily lives. While simply carrying on with daily life under often impossible circumstances can in itself be considered a form of non-violent resistance, more active forms of non-violent civil disobedience have also been inspired and informed by the concept of *sumud*, as evidenced, for example, by the Bethlehem activist and academic Mazin Qumsiyeh.

Since 1967, non-violent protests mounted by Palestinians, such as general strikes, boycotts and demonstrations, have been – and still are – associated with the concept of *sumud*. Professor Mazin Qumsiyeh is a profound believer in the visionary qualities of *sumud*, which he lives through his non-violent activism, but also in a deeper way:

> We could write volumes about resistance by simply living, eating, breathing in a land that is coveted. We resist by going to school, by cultivating what remains of our lands, by working under harsh conditions and by falling in love, getting married and having children. Resistance includes hanging onto what remains of Palestine when it has been made crystal-clear in words and deeds that we are not welcome in our lands.[38]

This deeper quality and potential of *sumud* was summed up recently by Toine van Teeffelen, after a conference on religious education held in Bethlehem in 2011, as describing two broad fields of values: on the one hand it refers to the values of being connected to the concrete Palestinian land, home and daily life, community, culture and identity; the value of a 'peaceful life under the olive tree' – the olive is a powerful symbol of *sumud* – appreciating the beauty and joy of life in spite of extremely adverse circumstances; keeping ecological harmony with earth and nature. On the other hand it also refers to broader human causes and communities, to the willingness to sacrifice and suffer if need be, serving the struggle for freedom and rights and the preparedness to keep going, to stay resilient like a cactus in the desert.[39]

Does this two-sided quality of *sumud* invite us again to the transfiguring quality of the mountain experience; an experience understood through the lens of the context of the demands being made on Jesus to commit to long-term suffering, humiliation and apparent failure, if he is to be faithful to the non-violent ministry with which he has been entrusted?

It is time to follow Jesus and take the road to the Holy City of Jerusalem.

Questions for reflection

1 The mystery of transfiguration engages our imagination as well as our hearts and minds. Jesus' three disciples wanted to build shelters, failing to recognize that in reality they had taken the next step toward the liberation of all of God's people. The movement from expecting a personal salvation to recognizing a shared responsibility challenges as readily as it supports discipleship. Spend time pondering any particular moments of transformation you have experienced and how they may have changed your way of being.

2 The Transfiguration is a *kairos* moment (see Chapter 4) where past, present and future coalesce. Recognizing that after his mountaintop experience Jesus 'set his face to go to Jerusalem', ask where you are in relation to living a costly discipleship: walking alongside or lurking behind? How do you now see Jesus' willingness to walk toward his inevitable death? What does it say about our need to engage in situations that may lead to personal suffering?

3 Palestinian economy, culture and sense of identity are inseparable from the olive tree as plant and as metaphor. The ongoing destruction of their olive groves is tantamount to an ethnic cleansing of a people. In Genesis we read that God sends Noah a dove with an olive branch as a sign that the floods have abated, right relationships (peace) have been restored (Genesis 8.11). Reread this story and reflect on how you might be a bringer of peace in the present situation. Is there some practical way in which you might contribute to the well-being of the olive growers? See <www.zaytoun.org> and <www.olivecoop.com>.

4   The Palestinian spirit of *sumud* is founded upon God's steadfastness and faithfulness as expressed by the psalmists and embodied by Jesus. It requires of the Palestinians a willingness to be humiliated and forbearing, and underpins their continued struggle against oppression by non-violent means of resistance (not to be confused with passivism). Does the ethic of non-violence challenge your way of thinking as a response to oppressive and/or totalitarian regimes? Where in your own life would the quality of *sumud* be found?

4

Confronting the truth: A redemptive journey of conversion

As he came near and saw the city, he wept over it, saying, 'If you, even you, had only recognized on this day the things that make for peace!'

Luke 19.41–42

In John 4, the divine gift of the Spirit breaks down barriers between peoples and leads to reconciliation and fellowship.   Judith Gundry-Wolf[1]

We begin the journey to the Holy City via a winding route – specifically, responding to the invitation of the Gospel of John to encounter the Samaritan woman at the well.[2] Jerusalem is the end point of our journey and it is vital to keep before our eyes the crucial importance of the Holy City for the three Abrahamic faiths of Judaism, Christianity and Islam – important not only for Israel/Palestine but for the rest of the world. Donald Nicholl's book, *The Testing of Hearts*, written as a diary when he was Rector of Tantur Ecumenical Institute, expressed Jerusalem's significance poignantly,[3] taking as inspiration an adaptation of Proverbs 17.3:

> For silver, the crucible,
> for gold, the furnace,
> *for the testing of hearts*,
> Jerusalem.

Jerusalem was his choice of city for the testing of hearts. We might want to add or substitute cities characterized by tragic conflicts such as Sarajevo, Baghdad, Damascus, Kabul, Kigali or Benghazi. However, Jerusalem is not only the city where the Israeli–Palestinian conflict is experienced at its most painful, the place where sacred shrines from the three faiths are situated – the Dome of the Rock (Islam), the Western Wall (Jewish – and on the site of the destroyed Temple) and the Church of the Holy Sepulchre (Christian, believed to be the site of Golgotha, where Jesus died)[4] – it is also fiercely desired by all three faiths as the capital of whatever new state will be formed. Sharing Jerusalem has always been a hugely contentious issue.

Starting point – Jacob's Well at Nablus

John gives us a different starting point for the journey of Jesus and the beginning of his ministry from the three Synoptic Gospels. After his baptism,[5] Jesus goes to the Galilee and performs his first 'sign'[6] in Cana, and then on to the Sea of Galilee (Capernaum), before returning to Judea where his disciples were baptizing. On deciding to return to Galilee he had to pass through Samaria. Samaria – or Sebaste – had been the capital of the northern kingdom before its destruction in 721 BCE.

It seems as if Jesus has deliberately chosen a historic site – Jacob's Well – for a contentious encounter. In Jesus' time, Jews did not speak to Samaritans, let alone Samaritan women. Although the origins of the Samaritans are shrouded in mystery (there are several conflicting theories), enmity between Jews and Samaritans had festered over the centuries and had probably begun at the time of the exile of the northern kingdom of Israel in 721 BCE.[7] But it became most evident at the time of the return of the Jews from exile in Babylon (535 BCE and after), when those who had stayed behind – the Samaritans – were accused of intermarriage, practising pagan religions, and thus of having become polluted. Not only this, but the Samaritans had resisted the programme of rebuilding the Temple in Jerusalem. As Willard Swartley says, 'Through these post-exilic decades and centuries, two contesting ideologies prevailed in Jewry: one more self-protective against outsiders . . . and another more inclusive of outsiders.'[8]

But the real schism between Jews and Samaritans occurred when Alexander the Great gave the Samaritans permission to build their own temple on Mount Gerizim: they believed the presence of God was experienced on the mountain, and that this had primacy over the Jewish Temple and ritual. The final split, which occurred after the Maccabean revolt, was a consequence of the brutal destruction of Samaritans by John Hyrcanus, who burned their temple on Mount Gerizim and destroyed Shechem (128 BCE). Small wonder these two communities avoided one another! Yet despite their dwindling numbers over 2,000 years, the custom of the Samaritans to ascend their holy mountain for important feasts has continued into the twenty-first century.

We will never know why Jesus chose Jacob's Well as a place of encounter. The actual well is not mentioned in the Old Testament, although Jacob's purchase of this piece of land at the city of Shechem is recorded.[9] But for this book's message of reconciliation, the meeting is vital. And how evocative of other contexts is this story of deepseated enmity with its roots in history. The tomb of Joseph – Qabr Yusuf – lies east of the village of Balata[10] (near the site of the ancient city of Shechem – Tell Balata), and the well is a little further east, about 2 kilometres from modern Nablus and reached through the Greek Orthodox monastery.[11] The meeting with the Samaritan woman reveals Jesus as the source of living water, water that gushes into eternal life. Not only does Jesus break social customs by talking with the woman, by lifting her from a position of ostracism to one of witness and mission, he emphasizes that the time for redemption is now – 'the hour is coming, and is now here' (John 5.25) – and that reconciliation occurs when boundaries of religion and history are broken, and true worshippers will worship in spirit and truth. Not by the ritual on Mount Gerizim or in the Temple at Jerusalem but in a way inclusive of all peoples at all times. This despised woman (who had chosen to come to the well for water in the heat of the day so as to avoid encounters with others), through her meeting with the exhausted Jesus becomes an evangelizer for her people, many of whom became believers, professing Jesus as Saviour. She is the first to receive the revelation that Jesus is the Messiah. Does she prefigure Martha, to whom Jesus reveals that he is 'the resurrection and the life'?[12] A Samaritan woman who has been wronged now becomes an agent of redemption. This is a rich text, summoning us to the mission of peacemaking and reconciliation: 'The sent one sends us, and beckons us to *go through Samaria*, offering the water of life that quenches the thirst of the human soul, and like an artesian spring, wells up unto eternal life.'[13]

It reminds us that the Easter Jesus will give the gift of peace at his first appearance to the disciples post-resurrection (John 20.19–20), but that this calling to peacemaking and reconciliation is already present from the earliest days of Jesus' ministry.

A journey of change and transformation

This story evokes the depth and ongoing nature of transformation that the Lenten pilgrimage requires. The woman changes radically because she has received the gift of compassionate listening and mercy. Jesus has cut through all outer pretences to bring into the spotlight the knowledge of the reality of her life. He will do the same to the accused prostitute (John 8) and to the woman of Luke 7, whose sins he forgave because of her great love. But he has also moved the focus of the encounter from personal conversion to one of mission and ministry – and is not this the challenge for today?

Reflecting what this could mean in the context of the Israeli–Palestinian conflict I thought about a recent journey I made to the former extermination camps of Auschwitz-Birkenau near Krakow in Poland. I was part of a group meeting to form policies against the trafficking of women and children.[14] Despite reading – even teaching – about the Holocaust/Shoah for many years, nothing can really adequately prepare for encountering the stark reality of the evil that was perpetrated at these grim sites. It reminded me of my visit to Rwanda, to genocide sites of the massacre of 1994, and the sight of the thousands of stacked skulls in the chapel of Ntarama, not far from the capital, Kigali.[15]

At Auschwitz I felt sorry for the guide who accompanied us round the site in the pouring rain: she had to tell this same grim story day after day, many times a day – pointing out not only the sites of gas chambers and ovens but personal objects, like the thousands of pairs of shoes, the children's clothes and the hundreds of photos chronicling the murderous procedures. The next day I visited Kazimierz, the old Jewish quarter near Krakow, trying to absorb what had once been a vibrant Jewish life in the city and what had been lost by Nazi extermination. It is completely understandable that Jewish collective memory is determined that the world will never forget what happened here, in the many other camps or the long tragic history of anti-Semitism, and how precious is the land of Israel in the rebuilding of Jewish life. But does not reconciliation also mean changing perceptions of the other, compassionate understanding of their suffering, and entering their world, however this conflicts with personal longstanding views – as Jesus did with the Samaritan woman?

And there *are* positive signs in this regard, namely some Jewish recognition of Palestinian suffering. For example, because of being confronted by ground realities, there has been an awakening to new consciousness, a willingness to understand the need for justice of all communities in the Bible lands. Some Jewish theologians have become critical of the way the Holocaust has been used. Norman Finkelstein, an American Jewish historian, has argued that the memory of the Holocaust has been exploited for political and financial gain to support the state of Israel. Israel, he wrote, 'one of the world's most formidable military powers, with a horrendous human rights record, has cast itself as a "victim" state'.[16]

Thus the Holocaust/Shoah has been used to justify the establishment of the state of Israel and to silence criticism against its unjust policies, instead of increasing the determination not to repeat its horrors by inflicting genocidal policies on the Palestinians.

Another example of a courageous, prophetic figure is Mark Braverman, an American Jewish psychotherapist who is now completely committed to peacemaking. Born in the USA in 1948, Braverman was raised in an amalgam of rabbinic Judaism and political Zionism. He was 'taught that a miracle – born of heroism and bravery – had blessed my generation. The state of Israel was not a mere historical event – it was redemption.' So when he first visited Israel as a boy of 17, he:

> fell in love with the young state. I was proud of the miracle of modern Israel . . . creating this vibrant country out of the ashes of Auschwitz. My Israeli family – religious Jews – warmly embraced me. But even as I embraced them in return, I heard the racism in the way they talked

about 'the Arabs'... I knew then that something was fundamentally wrong with the Zionist project, but my love for the Land stayed strong. After college, I lived for a year on a kibbutz, ignoring the implications of the pre-1948 Palestinian houses still in use and the ancient olive trees standing at the edges of its grounds.

In fact Braverman held fast to the Jewish narrative – until he went to the West Bank:

> Travelling in Israel and the Occupied Territories my defences against the reality of Israel's crimes crumbled. I saw the Separation Wall – I knew it was not for defence. I saw the damage inflicted by the checkpoints on Palestinian life and on the souls and psyches of my Jewish cousins in uniform who were placed there. I saw the settlements. I heard about the vicious acts of ideological Jewish settlers. And words like apartheid and ethnic cleansing sprang to my mind, unbidden and undeniable. And what is more, I learned that 1948, what I had learned to call The War of Liberation, was the *Nakba* – the ethnic cleansing of three-quarters of a million Palestinians from their villages, cities and farms. And I knew that what I was witnessing in the present, the whole apparatus of occupation, was a continuation of that project of colonization and ethnic cleansing. It horrified me and it broke my heart. Most important of all, I met the Palestinian people, and recognized them – no, claimed them – as my sisters and brothers. That summer, 40 years after my first encounter with the Land, I saw all that, and my relationship to Israel changed forever.[17]

A similar reaction is witnessed to by many Jewish thinkers and theologians (many are the children of Holocaust survivors), the most well-known being Marc Ellis.[18] Rabbi Michael Lerner, editor of the liberal Jewish journal *Tikkun* – *tikkun olam* means the 'healing of the world' – based in San Francisco, and who grew up in a Zionist household visited often by David Ben Gurion and Golda Meir, spent an extended time in a kibbutz in Israel at the age of 22. Though impressed, he was stunned by the lack of social ideals that were meant to be shaping political life in Israel:

> It was only when I began to ask about the origins of the kibbutz in the struggle against the Palestinian Arabs that I stumbled upon a terrible truth: the land on which I was working had been owned by Arabs who had been displaced by the Zionist enterprise.[19]

This discovery first set him on the search for peace and to start an organization called Committee for Peace in the Middle East. He continues to experience criticism and even personal attacks for his opposition to Zionist policies.[20] Yet another example is Sara Roy (now an authority on Gaza), a Jewish Harvard research scholar whose parents survived Buchenwald and Auschwitz. She went for research purposes to the West Bank and Gaza in 1985, and lived a summer that changed her life when she saw the humiliation of the Palestinian people and their treatment by the Israeli soldiers:

> It is perhaps in the concept of home and shelter that I find the most profound link between the Jews and Palestinians and, perhaps, the most painful illustration of the meaning of occupation . . . For Jews as for Palestinians, a house represents far more than a roof over one's head; it represents life itself.[21]

Along with these voices it is important to acknowledge many other Jewish initiatives for peace in Israel and beyond. For example, the growing activism of Jewish Voice for Peace, based in the USA, brings fresh hope. This is their recent statement condemning violence:

> Any act of violence, especially one against civilians, marks a profound failure of human imagination and causes a deep and abiding trauma for all involved. In mourning the nine lives lost in Gaza and the one life lost in Jerusalem this week, we reject the pattern of condemning the deaths of Israelis while ignoring the deaths of Palestinians. We do not discriminate. *One life lost is one life too many – whether Palestinian or Israeli.*[22]

No account would be complete without mention of the emergence of the Israeli 'revisionist' historians – including Ilan Pappé (mentioned in Chapter 1), Avi Schlaim, Benny Morris and Nur Masalha (not Israeli but a Palestinian Muslim).[23] What these historians share is that access to the historical archives has given insight and historical testimony to the truth of the Zionist aggression, especially events in 1948. In their different ways they have made a great contribution to altering consciousness, often at great cost to their personal lives.[24]

I also want to mention a shift in some Muslim thinking. A recent and promising development is the emergence of Islamic liberation theology. In his recent book, *Islamic Liberation Theology: Resisting the Empire*, Hamid Dabashi writes:

> What we are witnessing in much of the Muslim world today, as indeed in much of the world at large, is the rightful struggle of ordinary people for their pride of place, for social equanimity, economic justice, political participation, a legitimate and assertive place in the global redistribution of power.[25]

Beginning with a quote from the 'founding father' of liberation theology, Gustavo Gutiérrez, Dabashi declares that:

> 'In the last instance . . . we will have an authentic theology of liberation only when the oppressed themselves can freely raise their voice and express themselves directly and creatively in society and in the heart of the People of God, when they themselves "account for the hope," which they bear, when they are the protagonists of their own liberation.' For that to happen, that hope will have to transcend its particular (Jewish, Christian, Islamic, or any other) denominational divide and speak a metaphysics of liberation beyond the theology of one or another divisive claim on God. The particularity of that theology will have to speak a universal language, from the bosom of its particularity.[26]

This stance has been further elaborated in a Palestinian context. In June 2005, at the School of Oriental and African Studies in London, Dr Saied Reza Ameli[27] spoke of the universality of liberation theology. Building on the key concept that liberation theology is an attempt to liberate people of the world from poverty and oppression, he traced its relevance for the Palestinian people in specifically Islamic categories.[28] Its emergence is based on nostalgia for justice and nostalgia for metaphysical values.

Three elements are required. The first is return to God – this will affect our practices on the earth toward ourselves and others.[29] Second, selflessness – minimization of *personal desires* and dogmatic attachments to nationality, ethnicity and even religion are major requirements for caring for oppressed and poor people. This means avoiding all things that can be considered as 'selfishness'. 'Self' here is not only a person but can cover all 'collective centralities', such as Eurocentrism, Americocentrism and Zionism, which cause demolishing and destruction of 'others' for the price of supporting the 'self'. Furthermore:

Selflessness is a divine and mystical soul of all divine religions which brings God's spirit to all aspects of life . . . Here is where the Palestinian problem becomes a global issue for all human beings who care about 'others', here is the position at which 'all become equal to one and one becomes equal to all'; here is the position at which one can observe unity within diversity and diversity within unity.

Sumud equally challenges Palestinians with their responsibilities beyond their own situation.

The third element – common to all liberation theologies – is the centrality of justice. As regards Palestine, the relevance is that the 'Chosen society is the oppressed society' – referring to God's preference for the poorest and most vulnerable groups of people. As the Prophet Muhammad said: 'Shall I let you know about the kings of the Heaven? Every powerless deprived.' In Islam, he continues, the future is not in the hands of those who kept the powerless deprived. It is articulated as 'And We desired to show favour to those who were deprived in the land, and to make them Imams, and to make them the inheritors.'

This has a remarkable resonance with Christian hope from the foundational text, the Sermon on the Mount with its message that 'the meek will inherit the earth'. With this message of reconciliation that transcends the particularity of each religion, we have come full circle – back to Jesus' prophecy of a future when all will worship God 'in spirit and truth' (John 4.23).

Undertaking the redemptive journey

Like the Samaritan woman, we are commissioned to proclaim redemption and given the vocation of peacemaking. So how we understand Christ's journey as inspiring this vocation is vital. How were his actions redemptive and effective for today's situations of conflict? In other words, what do we mean by atonement today?

What we have already seen in the story of the woman at the well is the inseparability of justice-making from truth, and that these are both embodied in Jesus' lifestyle of suffering love, of non-violent resistance, in the struggle we are invited to share. In this struggle, what gives strength is the power of truth, the heart already reconciled to this truth. This is what makes our link today with Jesus setting his face to Jerusalem. His was the freely chosen path of suffering love, emerging from a being totally reconciled with the power and source of life and justice.

> So if anyone is in Christ, there is a new creation: everything old has passed away; see, everything has become new! All this is from God, who reconciled us to himself through Christ, and has given us the ministry of reconciliation. (2 Corinthians 5.17–18)

But Feminist Christology also stresses the *community* dimension of Christ's setting his face to confront the power of the system. Christ, together with the messianic community, embodied the struggle for truth and justice – even though the redemptive self-giving that led to his crucifixion was unique to Jesus. He – not his followers – is the saviour of the world. It is a mistake to idealize and glorify crucifixion, as some traditional theologies have done: this can so easily happen if the dimension of justice is removed. Putting justice central means there is a task for us all as we struggle anew against oppression in different contexts.

The non-violent struggle that appeared to end with crucifixion was a protest against all crucifixions, against the necessity of the violent putting to death of the innocent, poor and vulnerable. As Beverley Harrison wrote in a widely quoted passage:

> Jesus' death on a Cross, his sacrifice, was no abstract exercise in moral virtue. His death was the price he paid for refusing to abandon the radical activity of love . . . Sacrifice, I submit, is not a central moral goal or virtue in the Christian life. Radical acts of love . . . are the central virtues of the Christian moral life . . . Like Jesus, we are called to a radical activity of love, to a way of being in the world that deepens relation, embodies and extends community, passes on the gift of life . . . To be sure, Jesus was faithful unto death. He stayed with his cause and he died for it. He *accepted* sacrifice. But his sacrifice was *for* the cause of radical love, to make relationship and to sustain it, and, above all, to *righting* wrong relationship, which is what we call 'doing justice'.[30]

In a similar way, Rodolfo Cardenal SJ quotes his Jesuit colleague, Ignacio Ellacuría, murdered by Salvadoran soldiers, as saying: 'To liberate means to take the crucified people down from the Cross. But the world of oppression and sin cannot tolerate that the people be taken down from the Cross.'[31]

Those women who stood steadfast at the cross of Christ in the presence of the violence and brutality of the soldiers were ready to receive the empowerment of Christ's resurrection. We cannot escape the significance of the fact that these women disciples – like the Samaritan woman – had already experienced forgiveness and reconciliation within the community of those who struggled in suffering love for a new order of living. They had already accepted a ministry of peacemaking and reconciliation. Equally, their resistance to the established order was made possible because they were already empowered by Jesus' vision of a world graced with reconciliation.

A kairos *moment for Palestine*

It is time to leave the well at Nablus and take the road to Jerusalem. A *kairos* moment means a significant, historically decisive moment. Thus, as I write, the United Nations is about to meet in New York and to vote on the acceptance or rejection of Palestine as a state in its own right. There are arguments both for and against this proposal, the main argument against being the consequences of agreeing with a two-state solution for Israel/Palestine, as well as the difficulty of solving the refugee issue of the 'right of return'. Many – including Sabeel in Jerusalem – hope for a 'yes' vote so that there can be a break in the current deadlock. The current proposal can then form a basis for further negotiation. At present the outcome is still uncertain.

Whatever happens, this is a *kairos* moment for Palestine that was already flagged up by the Kairos Palestine Document, 'A Moment of Truth: A Word of Faith, Hope and Love from the Heart of Palestinian Suffering', in December 2009, promulgated in Bethlehem and written by a group of Christian clergy and lay people. The heart of this document is directly coherent with the content of Jesus' encounter with the Samaritan woman. This document, as Canon Naim Ateek wrote, is an attempt to challenge the theology of exclusivity and 'exceptionalism'.[32] Its theology is simple and straightforward:

We believe in a good and just God, who loves each one of [God's] creatures. We believe that every human being is created in God's image and likeness and that everyone's dignity is derived from the dignity of the Almighty One'. (2.2.1)

The document presents the ground realities simply and without exaggeration: 'Israeli settlements ravage our land in the name of God . . . Reality is the separation between members of the same family . . . Religious liberty is severely restricted' (1.1.2–4).[33]

The Palestinian Christian community is saying loudly and clearly – in both religious and political language – that the occupation is a sin and an evil (2.5; 3.1; 4.2.1). It criticizes any use of the Bible to legitimize or support injustice. It is also very clear that Palestinians are not against Israel or the Jewish people, but against the government that refuses to do justice and to make peace.

What is important for this non-violent understanding of atonement[34] is that the document is clear that 'Resistance is a right and a duty for the Christian. But it is *resistance with love as its logic*. It is thus a creative resistance for it must find human ways that engage the humanity of the enemy.' It urges '[s]eeing the image of God in the face of the enemy' (4.2.3) and suggests many practical ways of non-violent resistance. If the mission of the Samaritan woman was to evangelize her people, our task in today's redemptive journey to peace 'is a call to stand alongside the oppressed and preserve the word of God as good news for all' (6.1).[35]

Questions for reflection

1   The story of Jesus' contentious encounter with the Samaritan woman offers a paradigm of reconciliation between and within communities. The woman acknowledges her own frailty, accepts Jesus as the long awaited Messiah, *and* then evangelizes her neighbours. Do you see yourself as an evangelist, that is, a bringer of good news? Are you able to identify why this may seem an improbable idea? Equally, is it credible to imagine yourself as being an 'agent of redemption'? Take some time to reflect on these questions.

2   Church liturgy and hymnody frequently represent Jesus as 'victim', whereas Jesus' journey to the cross reveals him as a non-victim who actively travels toward inevitable suffering. Have there been occasions when you have adopted the role of 'victim'? How easy was it to recognize what was happening? Conversely, can you identify times when you have chosen the way of Jesus rather than collude with unjust systems?

3   Issues surrounding what for Palestinians is the colonization of their land are critical to the present Israel/Palestine. Take time to reflect on the conditional nature of God's promises to the Hebrew peoples, for example, Genesis 17.8–9; Leviticus 18.24–30; Leviticus 22.22–30.

4   Spend some time reading the Kairos Palestine Document, <www.kairospalestine.ps/sites/default/Documents/English.pdf>, then consider how you might share what you have learnt with your friends and/or in your faith community.

5

Resurrection as re-creation

—•◆•—

The Risen Christ says: 'In the depth of this reality I will speak, I will be present and I will transform.'   Rowan Williams[1]

Continuing the journey to the Holy City and specifically the journey of conversion begun in Chapter 4,[2] this chapter looks for glimpses of what resurrection hope will look like. How will the experience of risen life change our lives *now* and keep motivating us in the struggle for peace? This search will follow three stories from the Gospel of John, each shedding light on different aspects of the risen life that is the basis and hope of Christian faith. The unfolding sequence of stories leading to the climax of Jesus' suffering and death in Jerusalem suggests this approach: the Gospel for the Fourth Sunday of Lent is the story of the healing of the man born blind;[3] for the Fifth Sunday it is the raising of Lazarus, and the third story, the anointing of Jesus by Mary of Bethany, is read on Monday of Holy Week. Each story is revisited against the background of an escalation of fear and intimations of conspiracy and plotting to kill Jesus. Unlike the characters in the Gospel stories, today we have the advantage of knowing what will happen after the desolation of Calvary – that death did not have the last word. We share this conviction with the fledgling New Testament communities who read the stories seeking guidance and inspiration in their own turbulent times. Some of those communities would have had access to the memories of disciples who had lived through the events. So in line with the chosen lens of seeking answers for peace and conflict resolution in Israel/Palestine, we look for clues for change and transformation that will move us forward in today's struggles.

John's first-century community and the search for peace

First, there is a need to understand how the search for peace was experienced in John's Gospel and community. John, writing – it is thought – from a community in Asia Minor, perhaps Ephesus, unlike the writers of the Synoptic Gospels, does not tell us to 'love our enemies'. But his community is to be characterized by love: that is the way it will stand out against 'the world', by challenging those harmful values on which societies, then and now, are constructed – 'in John, love is the womb of Jesus' covenant of peace'.[4]

Resisting the temptation to understand John's references to 'the world' in a dualist way[5] or to see his negative references to 'the Jews' as anti-Semitic,[6] the focus here is on the 'life' and 'light' imagery that graces in abundance the community's life in Christ; it is also the escalating injunction to live the ethic of love and of loving service, of which Jesus' journey toward Calvary is prototype and inspiration.

Second, living the ethic of love is far from limited to personal relationships but has community, moral and political dimensions. Many contemporary communities are inspired by this ethic of love, and a specific example would be the Catholic Worker Communities founded in American cities in the twentieth century by the peace activist Dorothy Day.[7] About 80 houses in total were founded – welcoming poor vagrants and people made homeless for a variety of reasons. It is in the combination of loving service and political protest that the inspiration to love was lived out in Catholic Worker houses. Dorothy herself was a very 'hands on' person in terms of making exhausted people comfortable with pillows, books, music and cups of hot tea or soup. She knew that beauty was an ingredient of healing.[8] When someone asked how long people were permitted to stay, she answered:

> We let them stay forever ... They live with us, they die with us, and we give them a Christian burial. We pray for them after they are dead. Once they are taken in, they become members of the family. Or rather, they always were members of the family. They are our brothers and sisters in Christ.[9]

But a person of deep prayer, she was deeply involved with political protests against racism (with Martin Luther King), nuclear arms (she influenced the Bishops of the Second Vatican Council and was a friend of Thomas Merton), against the root causes of poverty and injustice – and always joined in or initiated marches for peace. Of course this meant facing imprisonment. There are no boundaries to love, and Dorothy Day continues to inspire the contemporary peace movement.

So the boundaries of Church–world are always permeable and discourage us from taking the kind of elitist and dualist 'faith versus society' stance adopted by some sectarian Churches. Jesus – also in John's Gospel – is confronting people on the margins of society, such as the Samaritan woman[10] and the adulterous woman of John's Gospel (chapter 8). Even if John's Christology is often called a 'high Christology', this Jesus a 'divine' Jesus, yet this Jesus is also divinity enfleshed and embodied, who understands the human need to be fed and healed, and, more significantly, to love and to be loved in a community calling itself 'beloved' because it is called by God into being and relationship. Peace was the gift of the risen Jesus to his disciples,[11] and love was the command to Peter on the shores of Galilee – movingly depicted in the painting in the Church of St Peter in Gallicantu, Jerusalem.[12] This unbroken love flowing from God to Jesus to his followers is the inspiration for an abiding non-violent covenant of peace.

The healing of the man born blind: creation revisited[13]

We are invited to join Jesus and his followers on the streets of the Holy City. It is the Sabbath day – a day set aside for remembering and celebrating creation. But there is also a background of mounting conflict and plotting against Jesus. We are told that anyone confessing Jesus as Messiah will be expelled from the Synagogue.[14] The scene of the healing of the man born blind will alternate between the Temple and the Pool of Siloam, which was not far from the cistern or pit of Jeremiah (north of Damascus Gate).[15] The Pool of Siloam is vital for this journey, not only because of the story here but because of the importance of water in the history of salvation then and now, of the part water plays in the Palestine/Israeli conflict.

The Pool of Siloam – we are told this means 'sent' – has been regarded as sacred by a variety of faiths since ancient times. Jews used water from the pool for purification rituals in the Temple during the Feast of Tabernacles, and it was probably the site of the pagan Shrine of the Four Nymphs built by Hadrian in 135 CE. Christians were naturally drawn to the pool as a site of pilgrimage because of John's story, and its healing properties are mentioned in the journals of the earliest pilgrims, such as the Bordeaux (333 CE) and Piacenza (sixth century) pilgrims. But the Pool of Siloam visited by these Byzantine pilgrims was probably the one next to Hezekiah's tunnel with the same name, and may not have been the one actually bathed in by the blind man.

Ancient records report that during the Second Temple period there was a *lower* pool. In the summer of 2004, archaeologists were checking the area south-east of the traditional Pool of Siloam for a public works project when they discovered some large stone steps: further excavations uncovered several flights of steps and a pool that was in use during the first century CE. Could this be the real Pool of Siloam? This small pool collected some of the water as it emptied there at the southern end of Hezekiah's tunnel. The water would continue on through a channel into the recently discovered pool. The source of the water is the Gihon Spring located at the northern end of Hezekiah's tunnel, on the eastern side of the City of David. Much more of the pool remains to be excavated, and this currently lies under a beautiful garden, in fact an orchard, known as the King's Garden, owned by the Greek Orthodox Church.

What John relates here is a story of re-creation: it is a powerful 'mini-Gospel' in its own right. At first sight it appears to offer the familiar scenario of an 'Amazing Grace' variety ('I was blind but now I see'), understanding Jesus' compassionate response to the blind man as symbolic of a deeper conversion of faith. One problem rears its head here before we go further. As theologian John Hull explains, from the profundity of his own personal experience of blindness, the Gospels harp on blindness as symptomatic of lack of faith, of unwillingness to hear and see the truth. It is very painful for sight – or hearing – impaired people to discover their impairment being used in Scripture to symbolize lack of faith and moral blindness.

John Hull, in his 'Open Letter from a Blind Disciple to a Sighted Saviour', writes:

> Dear Jesus,
>
> According to the Gospel of Matthew, you used the expression 'blind' as a term of abuse. When you were attacking certain groups of people you described them as 'blind guides' (Mt. 23:16), 'blind fools' (v.17), and 'you blind Pharisee' (v.26). You have given your authority to those down the ages who have disparaged others through references to visual loss. Whenever a Member of Parliament criticises a government minister by saying that he or she shows a blind disregard for the welfare of the people of this country, whenever a sports journalist describes a cricketer as having struck out blindly with the bat, or an academic recommends blind marking, the impression is reinforced that blind people are stubborn, callous, lacking in self-control or just plain igno-rant. It would have been so easy for you to have called them 'careless guides', 'stupid fools', or 'stubborn Pharisees'. If you had spoken in that way, then the disparaging image of blindness, which has caused blind people so much pain, would not have received your permission and encouragement.[16]

He finds similar difficulties with the story under discussion here:

> Your disciples anticipated a connection between disability and sin with the question 'who did sin, this man or his parents, that he was born blind?' You rejected this suggestion, adding 'that God's works might be revealed in him' (v.3). In other words, the man had been blind from birth not because of some parental sin but in order to create a sort of photo opportunity for you, my Lord. When you spoke of God's works being revealed in the blind man, you were not referring to his blindness, but to the restoration of his sight. The implication is that God's works cannot be seen in a blind person but only in a blind person becoming sighted.[17]

But how can that be a saving and healing message to those who remain blind all their lives? The climax of the story in the evangelist's telling of it is that Jesus accuses the Pharisees of claiming to see, when actually they are blind. So the sin lies not in the literal blindness but in *the self-deception of those who believe that they have insight but do not*. If this conclusion gives John Hull no comfort, he does find some nourishment later, during the Passion narrative:

> As I read your gospels, thinking about these problems, I come upon
> a passage which I have known all my life, but it has never struck me
> before how relevant it is to my present life as a blind person. After they
> had tried and sentenced you to . . . death, the servants of the High Priest
> began to spit on you, blindfold you and strike you, saying 'Prophesy!
> Who hit you?' (Mk. 14:65).

Whereas he realizes that to be blindfolded is not to be blind and to
be a sighted person who cannot see is not the same as to be a blind
person, yet Jesus' experience of being *blind* folded begins to come
close to it. In asking whether, in these moments of de facto blindness,
Jesus began to know blindness from the inside and whether his own
words, 'blind fools!' came back to him, strangely, Hull's indignation
begins to die away and his questions are silenced. Jesus has become
a partner in the world of blindness, one who shares his condition.
He has become a 'blind brother'.

John Hull's insights offer yet another lens through which to read
the text of Scripture: so many of Jesus' words address those who
refuse either to see or hear – those who harden their hearts, reject
the message and turn their backs. Can we press the meaning further
to offer a more generous inclusive vision to creation that touches
our present situation? I think Jesus recalls not only the blind man
but all humankind to the moment of creation, and thus to the
possibility of re-creation. Remember the previously mentioned
Jewish mystical insights,[18] that through meditation and spiritual
practices the power of the creation can be brought into the
present. Meditating in this way means attempting to experience a
connection to the life and sacred power of the creation moment.
John has already described Jesus telling us that 'no one can enter
the kingdom of God without being born of water and Spirit',[19] and
Christians have connected this with sacramental baptism. Jesus uses
both earth and water for this moment of re-creation. For listeners
then and now this evokes the creation of the universe when the
Spirit was hovering over the waters[20] – but evokes it as present
invitation and command. 'Go and wash,' the blind man was told.
And in the final encounter with Jesus the moment of revelation is
given him, that Jesus is the Son of Man – and he worships him. This
is the climax to which the gift of restored sight is leading. But there

is another creation story behind this text, and that is of the vision of Isaiah 6.1.

Texts of the prophet Isaiah are often referred to as the Fifth Gospel, so redolent is the New Testament with his ideas, inspiration and imagery.[21] Because John (12.37–43) refers to Isaiah three times, in the context of the unbelief of the people, it is likely that Isaiah's words lie behind our passage. The prophet's text appealed to is a heartbreakingly beautiful one, where Isaiah has a vision of God's glory, of God enthroned in the heavenly court, probably the vision that defined his whole life and ministry, inspiring his visions of re-creation of humanity and nature.[22] Integral to it is Isaiah's response, 'Here I am, send me!' (Keep in mind that the Pool of Siloam means 'sent'.) Yet here again we have the troubling words that God commands him to tell the people:

> 'Keep listening, but do not comprehend;
> keep looking, but do not understand.'
> Make the mind of this people dull,
> and stop their ears.   (Isaiah 6.9–10)

Is it possible that what both the Genesis and Isaiah texts reflect is the tragic fact that in one set of stories, Genesis, God offered the richness and blessedness of creation in all its diversity, but humanity exploited this gift? In Isaiah's story, the prophet's call is set within a vision of a Creator passionately caring about Creation within the knowledge of what humanity has done to it and of the purification needed to be an effective and authoritative witness. True, blindness and deafness are used as models of faithlessness, but the deepest criticism is that they do not 'comprehend with their minds'. In the story of the man born blind, it is significant, first, that he has been *born* blind, so has to be returned to origins, to the point of re-creation in the kingdom of God. Second, he is re-created with a mission: as a believer, not only are his eyes and ears opened but, far more significantly, his heart has accepted the truth.

And is not this also the message for us, in the context of conversion to the truth of Israel/Palestine? Our hearts must open to hear and understand the truth of all peoples living in the land. Truth is where the symbolism of light leads us. And the mission that the blind man was given – and that we inherit – is that to be reborn in water and the Spirit is to accept the vocation and ministry to understand that truth is complex. To understand the pain, suffering and historical memories of two peoples, both Israelis and Palestinians, in the longest-lasting conflict in the Middle East, with ramifications spread throughout the whole of the region, is to enter more deeply into the fullest meaning of resurrection, risen life: it is to accept the challenge to enter empathically into the truth of the other, even the hostile other.

'Lazarus, come forth!'

The second story, the raising of Lazarus (John 11.1–57), takes us out of the Holy City, to Bethany, even nearer to the last days of Jesus and the mystery of death-to-life. The sense of danger is escalating: the disciples are horrified when Jesus suggests returning to Judea: 'Rabbi, why would you want to go there – the last time they tried to stone you!'[23] And the result of the raising of Lazarus is that 'from that day on they planned to put him to death' (11.53).

This story is cherished partly because of the special relationship of Jesus to the family of Lazarus, Martha and Mary (he loved them all intensely), and partly because of the dramatic essence of the story itself and its relationship with Jesus' own resurrection. Traditionally Bethany has been identified with the village of Al-Eizaria in the West Bank. Al-Eizaria in Arabic means 'Place of Lazarus', the reputed site of the Tomb of Lazarus – although the identification is by no means certain – and about 2.4 kilometres to the east of Jerusalem on the south-eastern slope of the Mount of Olives (or higher up, closer to Bethpage). The Israeli Security Wall comes very close, with all that this means for the lives of contemporary villagers, both Muslim and Christian. Visiting recently, I experienced a sense of desolation here that brings the misery of the occupation closer. Poverty was visible and multiple enormous rubbish heaps reinforced the reality that this village lacked basic amenities.

Notwithstanding, Bethany occupies a key place in our narrative, not only for this story and the anointing story that follows but because Jesus in the week before his arrest in Jerusalem would withdraw to the Mount of Olives and possibly to Bethany each night.[24] Much dispute has arisen as to the meaning of 'Bethany':[25] St Jerome – following a Syrian source – thought it meant 'House of Affliction', relating to the use of the village as a centre for caring for the sick and aiding the destitute and pilgrims to Jerusalem (we know that Jesus had dinner at the house of Simon the Leper in Bethany).[26] It is also possible that the village had Essene connections – and was one of the three designated villages for those Essenes to stay, for example lepers, who were considered too ritually impure to enter Jerusalem. One theory is that a poor-house:

> was established at Bethany to intercept and care for pilgrims at the end of the long and potentially arduous journey from Galilee. The house combined this work with care for the sick and destitute of the Jerusalem area. Thus Bethany received its name because it was the Essene poor-house par excellence, the poorhouse that alleviated poverty closest to the Holy City.[27]

So Jesus, knowing he walks into danger, deeply distressed at his friend's sickness-unto-death, journeys to Judea and to Bethany. This story loves ambiguities! Jesus is upset, yet delays three days. Lazarus is not dead, but sleeping. Lazarus will rise – but now, or on the last day? Grief is everywhere – the sisters weep, the Jews present weep and Jesus weeps. As with the story of the healing of the man born blind, the confession of faith elicits a revelation from Jesus. In the previous story it was Jesus as Son of Man. Here it is Martha's belief in Jesus that prompts his revelation as the resurrection and the life, and her subsequent confession of faith in him as Messiah. Jesus is deeply disturbed in spirit: this conflict is one at the deepest level – with the powers of evil. It is almost as if it plays out as a trial of the week that is to come. Lazarus is summoned back to life through the unity of God and Jesus: as in our previous story, the glory of the God of creation is revealed by the re-creation of Lazarus.

But what does this mean for our theme? Lazarus will die again, at his appointed hour. But we are to live from resurrection faith – and from the gift of this story. Wherever the story of Lazarus is told, it is with the meaning of transformed consciousness. For example, Morris West's novel, *Lazarus*, tells of an imaginary Pope, Leo XIV – almost at death's door with heart disease caused by excessive eating and drinking, but also at risk from both Islamic and Israeli terrorists – who is offered the gift of physical new life by skilled surgery.[28] But he had always been a dominating and feared figure, blocking change and progress, without an ounce of compassion. The near brush with death transforms him so that when, finally, he is the victim of the terrorist's gun, he is a changed human being.

My second example is closer to the theme of this book. One of the most moving passages of Dostoevsky's *Crime and Punishment* is where the murderer, Raskolnikoff, and the prostitute, Sonia (actually a saintly figure), read together the story of the raising of Lazarus. As yet Sonia is unaware of Raskolnikoff's guilt.[29] She reads the story with great emotion and stops after the words, 'Then many of the Jews who came to Mary . . . believed in him': 'The dying piece of candle lit up this low-ceilinged room in which an assassin and a harlot had just read the Book of Books.'[30]

A long process is now set in motion where, through Sonia's deep love, Raskolnikoff is brought to the point of public confession and repentance for his crime: '"Yes," said Raskolnikoff with a smile, "I am come to bear the Cross, Sonia."'[31]

And he goes to the market place, where the crowd is thickest, kisses the ground, and in everyone's presence, confesses himself a murderer. He is sentenced to Siberia for seven years, but there the writer ends, with a new story of regeneration, 'a change from one world to another'.[32]

This is what the Lazarus story offers: living from the ethic of redemptive love, our consciousness can be transformed. New levels of empathy can be reached. Sonia, though profoundly shocked at the crime Raskolnikoff had committed, never saw him as beyond redemption. Duncan Macpherson, preaching about this story, hears the words 'Lazarus, come forth!' as Jesus speaking to all of us:

> he speaks out for all who are unjustly imprisoned and bound and in our world all the forces of oppression and injustice that afflict his sisters and brothers – and he tells any who will listen to "Take the stone away".[33]

Rabbi Michael Lerner, in *Embracing Israel/Palestine*, considers that both communities, Israelis and Palestinians, are suffering from post-traumatic stress disorder (PTSD). He writes:

From this Jewish perspective, we have never completed the psychological work needed to recover from our profound experience of humiliation and suffering so that we can instead experience righteous indignation at anyone who turns the powerless Other into a victim.[34]

Is this where the Lazarus experience pushes us? Into being open to painful places where transformed consciousness wants to bring us?

The Bethany anointing[35]

We are again at Bethany, at the home of the two sisters and Lazarus. The atmosphere of danger is ever present: at the end of this story, Lazarus' (newly restored) life will also be under threat from the authorities. This story of Mary of Bethany anointing Jesus' feet with costly perfume and wiping them with her hair is greatly loved and offers new insights in this quest for peace. It is also puzzling. Has John conflated the three anointing stories, that of Mark (also at Bethany in the House of Simon the Leper),[36] where an unnamed woman anoints the *head* of Jesus, a prophetic gesture, and the story in Luke 7, where an unnamed woman 'of the town' anoints the *feet* of Jesus, wipes them with her hair and is forgiven because 'she loved much'?[37] Christian tradition has certainly confused the three stories, so that the woman in Luke 7 becomes (mistakenly) identified with Mary of Magdala. Instead of understanding her as a woman healed by Jesus, then a disciple and witness to the resurrection, western tradition persists in regarding her as a repentant prostitute. Mary of Bethany is also confused with her, despite the tradition, also known by Luke,[38] that she was close to Jesus, both respected and loved by him. Admittedly, her action in letting down her hair and wiping Jesus' feet does not seem characteristic!

Leaving aside these puzzles, the story as we have it in our text is important in many ways for this journey. First, recall that it was suggested above that there was a house for the poor and sick here – so Jesus' words (which at first glance appear uncaring), 'The poor you have always with you', can be understood in this context. Second, the story reveals the dimension of mutuality in the redemptive story. Focusing exclusively on Jesus as Redeemer – which he is – may obscure the part necessary for all followers to play, and especially today. Jesus does not stop history! But he did understand and receive the significance of Mary's extravagant gesture! Which of us, caring for an extremely sick or dying relative, would not hesitate to buy beautiful flowers, a piece of music or even something attractive to wear in bed – unnecessary, but wanting to express how much this person means to us? Mary knew, intuitively, that Jesus' death was close and chose to honour and reverence what he meant to the community.

This highlights what is sometimes understressed: women's role in the redemptive story and contribution to the idea of non-violent atonement (referred to in Chapter 4),[39] namely that God's way of saving the world and reversing the ethic of violent conflict as a way to solve all disputes is the way of non-violence and non-retaliation.[40] This is why John's ethic of love is no fuzzy command but a counter-cultural way of being to a world 'thriving' on hatred and revenge. Luke's Gospel told us of women following Jesus and ministering to him from their own resources.[41] Becoming disciples in the messianic community offered women a liberating role in New Testament times, since they were valued outside the trammels of traditional patriarchy. That fact has sometimes obscured women's contribution to living out the redemptive role of non-violence. Standing by the cross of Jesus was both a political act and a high form of resistance and should be recognized as such. It is an act exemplifying relational and mutual energy: standing by the cross, the women found the strength, the focused attention, to 'stand with', 'withstand' the situation, with the necessary openness and vulnerability to 'receive' Easter morning.[42] It is redemptive, because symbolic of the way God is present to suffering and oppression. God is a God of compassion – 'suffering with' – and at the same time, opening up new possibilities for a transformed future.

What these three stories have shown, in the context of Palestinian occupation, is that the grace of resurrection can be the source and resource for living now: the language of redeeming grace is the language of claiming the non-violent power of relating – the only true path to save the world. But for Jesus there was no short-circuiting the path of suffering and death. To this we must now turn.

Questions for reflection

1 The three Gospel stories accompanying us on our journey toward resurrection are set against a background of escalating fear. What in each of these stories might help you in personal fear-filled situations? Are you able to share any insights within your group or with a trusted friend?

2 A common 'urban' myth of today is that religion and politics should not mix. Take time to reflect on how this can be a valid assertion in the light of John's Gospel and its intrinsic 'ethic of love'. Where in your own church community do you see this ethic at work, and if not, why not?

3 How did you respond to John Hull's challenge to Jesus as a 'blind disciple'? Against this background consider any current use and abuse of language in our society, especially in relation to disability. Are there any ways in which you experience prejudice or bias? Are you aware of times when you express or suppress prejudice or bias? Take these to God in prayer.

4 Mary of Bethany expresses her willingness to be vulnerable. Set aside time to reread her story (John 12.1–11.) As you read, ask for the grace to understand how God might be answering your search for holy living, for re-creation.

6

Walking the Via Dolorosa

All cities are windows into foreign mindsets but this one is also a two-way mirror revealing her inner life while reflecting the world outside. Whether it was the epoch of total faith, righteous empire-building, evangelical revelation or secular nationalism, Jerusalem became its symbol, and its prize.   Simon Sebag Montefiore[1]

The Jerusalem I was raised to love was the terrestrial gateway to the divine world where Jewish, Christian and Muslim prophets, men of vision and a sense of humanity, met – if only in the imagination.

Sari Nusseibeh[2]

Jerusalem was the destination Jesus chose to confront the combined religious and secular power and might of Rome, Judea and Galilee, even though his active ministry had been focused on Galilee – and we do not even know how many times he had actually been to Jerusalem. That this journey would result in his death was inevitable, given the destabilizing nature of his activities in Galilee. Jerusalem is also the place – as mentioned earlier – where the contemporary Arab/Israeli conflict is experienced just as acutely as in the West Bank – although the poverty levels and deprivation of Arab communities here are not yet as desperate as in Gaza. Here I link the past voluntary suffering and redemptive love of Jesus with the contemporary suffering of the Arab communities through the motif of the Via Dolorosa. This, the 'Path of Suffering' or 'The Sorrowful Journey', is the way Christians through the ages have chosen to remember the last days and hours of Jesus of Nazareth, even if the actual journey today bears little relation to what actually happened in first-century Palestine. Bargil Pixner writes:

> Every Friday afternoon a procession of Catholic believers reverently
> singing a processional hymn leave the al-Omariya School, the place of
> the former fortress Antonia, to make their way toward the Church of the
> Holy Sepulchre located within the Old City Walls of Jerusalem ...
> The Franciscans ... lead the weekly procession in Jerusalem through
> the narrow streets of the Muslim quarter on a route called the Via
> Dolorosa.[3]

He explains that the route followed today has such a venerable tradition that it would be unthinkable to change it. Yet there are elements
that are completely unhistorical. So how does today's devotional
path relate to the route Jesus took, and how does this affect the contemporary conflict situation? The position taken in this chapter is
that the Via Dolorosa acts as a metaphor linking past and present,
and we can enter into it on many levels. The first is to try to understand the historical pressures on Jesus and his passage (*transitus*) from
self-giving, redemptive suffering and death to resurrection – and,
as preface to this, the Via Dolorosa of tradition is briefly revisited.
Our journey will begin on the Mount of Olives and end at the traditional site of Golgotha, now believed to be part of the revered Church
of the Holy Sepulchre.

Second, this is the non-violent journey to redemption that
Jesus made in a world as enslaved by violence now as it was in his
own times. I explore how the dynamic of non-violence, and redemption seen as *making right relation*, was embodied by Jesus, inspiring
the breakthrough to resurrection and the risen life for us all. But
this is not just a revisitation of the past: it is an invitation to follow
and embrace this dynamic in our own lives today, mindful that
Jesus is the Saviour who blazed the trail for us to follow. So,
third, the Via Dolorosa is revisited, making links with the suffering
of Palestinians today – as well as other conflictual situations in
the wider Middle East. On all of these levels, redemption as right
relation attempts to include all parties in the conflict, identifying
flashpoints where hatred is giving way to positive movements
toward reconciliation. We end at the traditional site of Golgotha,
in the Church of the Holy Sepulchre, in the interstitial space of Holy
Saturday, then a time of desolation, now a time of grief yet framed
with hope.

The Via Dolorosa revisited

Some of the problems of revisiting the Via Dolorosa are illustrated by our starting point: the Mount of Olives. In 1859 Edward Lear, the English water-colour painter, writer and poet, painted a beautiful picture of Jerusalem at sunrise from the Mount of Olives.[4] In the foreground a group of nomadic shepherds – Bedouin? – are looking toward the walls of the Holy City: both the Temple Mount itself and the city are devoid of the frenzied activity of the building of churches that would follow in the next few decades. There is a haunting beauty in the rural emptiness of the hillside – a reminder that one of Jerusalem's glories is the alternation between rural and city geographies, between wilderness and densely populated areas, both rich with story and spiritual meaning.[5] There is plenty of evidence of earlier churches and monastic communities on this site from the fourth century onwards, but by the nineteenth century – when Lear and others like the Scottish painter David Roberts[6] contemplated this view – there was little left, except ruins and gardens.[7] Even if this would all change in the next 50 years, the Mount still engenders an atmosphere of brooding over sacred memories, a sense of connection with yet separation from the complexity of the city's life. And above all, it carries both the memory of Jesus weeping over the city, a memory enshrined in the stones of the Dominus Flevit Church,[8] and the site of the Garden of Gethsemane where he underwent his moment of greatest trial. From this small church – Dominus Flevit – there is the same glorious vista toward the city that Lear's nomadic shepherds were enjoying.

So even if the route of the Via Dolorosa has changed several times in history, the beginning point – the Garden on the Mount of Olives – and the end point at Golgotha remain constant. The Via Dolorosa pilgrimage began in the middle of the fourth century, as soon as it became safe for Christians to walk openly this pilgrim way, after the Emperor Constantine made Christianity the official religion of the Roman Empire. Originally, Byzantine pilgrims followed a similar path to the one taken today but did not stop along the way. Over the centuries the route has changed several times even if, today, the main route of the Via Dolorosa is that of the early Byzantine pilgrims, with 14 stations along the way. Alternative routes are followed by those who have different opinions on the locations of various events, but for most pilgrims the exact location of each event along the Via Dolorosa is of little importance. For example, it does not now seem very significant that the Praetorium – where Jesus would have been tried by Pontius Pilate – was not in the Fortress Antonia but nearer today's Jaffa Gate, where Herod the Great had built a fortress for himself and his family. It is the *spiritual* meaning of being close to the site of original events, and reflecting on them for the enrichment of faith today, that is the point.[9]

There is a linked historical difficulty in that some of the events of the Via Dolorosa are unmentioned by the four Gospel accounts, such as the story of Veronica wiping the face of Jesus, the three falls of Jesus, as well as his meeting with his mother Mary. All of these events have acquired great spiritual meaning – if not historical veracity – over the centuries. In addition, there is a deeper historical question as to the path we follow: how could the Gospel writers know so much about the details of Jesus' trial, condemnation and death? That Jesus was crucified has been confirmed by sources external to Scripture like the Jewish historian, Josephus.[10] But by their own admission, the followers of Jesus were terrified: they fell asleep in the Garden of Gethsemane as he underwent his greatest trial, and fled from the process of his carrying his cross and death, the women standing by the cross being the sole exception, according to the Synoptic Gospels.[11] How could they claim to know so much about what happened? We know that the Roman regime's intention was to inspire terror through using crucifixion as a punishment. Not only was it an agonizing and humiliating death, but crucifixion brought further dishonour because it was virtually impossible to bury the body. Dominic Crossan points out that only one crucified skeleton has been discovered from all the thousands that the Romans murdered in this way. Crossan writes grimly, 'if you seek the heart of darkness, follow the dogs'.[12] He means that because of the lurking dogs and carrion crows, there would be little of the person left to bury. This was all a deliberate part of the dishonour: as we know from contemporary liberation struggles, families deprived of the dead body of a loved one find the sorrow far harder to endure. Of course there were occasions when the soldiers would hasten the process of dying, so it could happen that a person might be released to his family for burial. We will never know exactly the truth of what happened to Jesus at the time of his death, but one thing is certain: the terror of crucifixion lies behind the sacred texts.

Consequently, this means that if the texts as we read them are not even trying to be accurate historical narratives, what are they trying to convey? What Crossan suggests is that we have here 'not *history remembered* but *prophecy historicized*'.[13]

In no way is this trying to undervalue the Gospels: on the contrary, what it shows us is that the early Christian communities saw in the whole Christ event the fulfilment of what so much Scripture had been foretelling. It was not only the cross and resurrection that were important but the entire life of Jesus of Nazareth, beginning with the way his birth was foretold by an angel and his pre-existence with God. So they combed Scripture for profounder meanings and understandings – inspired perhaps by the way the risen Jesus had instructed the two disciples on the way to Emmaus.[14] And of course, as indicated earlier, particular appeal was made to the prophet Isaiah to illuminate the fuller meaning of redemption. But this was a post-resurrection process and does not reflect the self-understanding of Jesus in his own lifetime.

So the invitation now is to walk the Via Dolorosa, seeking the unfolding of its hidden meanings for peace and reconciliation for us today.

The Via Dolorosa – a non-violent path to redemption

From the walls of the Dominus Flevit Church on the Mount of Olives, looking out to the walls of the Holy City, the challenge is to reread the story as we are given it, to reinspire and re-create hope in the current impasse in Israel/Palestine. Jesus' Galilean ministry has been understood as one of healing, as a call to a non-violent discipleship within the dream of the kingdom of God, where justice and peace will ultimately triumph. From the beginning, Jesus has been embodying the way of non-violence. He has not joined the groups of Zealots, who were the political rebels against the Roman regime in the region. He has not opposed the Roman tax system but rather invited the local tax collector to join his community and inspired another, Zacchaeus, to make restitution for his fraudulent activities.[15] Yet he clearly offended local leaders by his insistence on open table fellowship: 'he eats with tax collectors and sinners (= prostitutes)' was the frequent accusation. This was only one way of his resisting an oppressive status quo.

The way of non-violent resistance is sometimes mocked as weak and passive, but this is far from the truth. The Palestinian scholar-activist Mazin Qumsiyeh in his life and work demonstrates the profundity of its methods in contemporary times: 'How many in the West have heard of the women's movement of the 1920s against the British occupation and its support of colonial Zionism?'[16]

From the 1920s and 1930s, women took the initiative at critical times and also in the post-1967 years when the national will was debilitated. For example, the first demonstration in spring 1968 was led by women – and dispersed by force. Similarly in 1968, over 300 women in Gaza demonstrated about the policies of occupation, expulsions and land confiscations.[17]

For Mazin Qumsiyeh, like Jesus, Gandhi, Martin Luther King, Aung San Suu Kyi and John Dear,[18] this focus on non-violent resistance is crucial.[19] Whereas state power is brilliant at *mobilizing* fear, *shedding* fear is vital for maintaining alternative possibilities. Hence these prophetic figures are frequently drawn on to inspire the heart of non-violent resistance and the *sumud* of the people – referred to earlier.[20] This stance permeates every aspect of existence. It is both an ideal and a practical way of living. Qumsiyeh has already been cited in Chapter 3 about the dimension of *sumud* embodied in the courage of simply keeping alive the ordinary dimensions of life. This is resistance in its most fundamental meaning. It also includes hanging onto what is left of cherished Palestinian land.[21]

This captures the way of being of Jesus in the villages and shores of Galilee – a stance issuing from the very fibre of his being, calling out to the world for a response of solidarity, for transformation of consciousness and action.

What underlies Jesus' path along the Via Dolorosa is a vision of redemption as right relation. We have seen above that state power inspires terror – understandably, if the end of the road is crucifixion. There are two Greek words for power in the New Testament, *dunamis* and *ousia*. *Ousia* means that institutional power given with a position of authority, granted by state-supported institutions. *Dunamis*, relational power, is more fluid and more difficult to define. It is also fragile. Yet it is this power, driven by the passion for justice, that drove Jesus throughout his Galilean ministry; that is the driving redemptive force toward his death and resurrection.[22] First, relational power, or the power of mutuality-in-relation, is a power that brings to birth existing potential in the way Jesus was constantly empowering his followers to heal, exorcize and preach the kingdom, but emphasizing the dependence of this power on deep faith.[23] Second, relational power is the power of awareness, sensitivity and empathy, affiliation and bonding – all part of the power of compassion (to understand compassion as 'pity' is to miss its relational element). Compassion in its root meaning is 'to bear', to 'withstand'. The theologian Carter Heyward wrote that compassion is:

> to bear up God in the world. To withstand or 'stand with' God is 'to be in solidarity with God' . . . to go with God in our comings and goings. This vocation involves pain, as Jeremiah, Jesus and all bearers of God have known, but not only pain. To be passionate lovers of human beings, the earth, and other earth creatures; to love passionately the God who is Godself, the resource of this love is to participate in an inspired and mind-bogglingly delightful way of moving collectively in history.[24]

This power of compassion is rooted in the creative passion of God seeking to bring to birth these new dynamics of relating. It is the power that drives to healing and wholeness, even the power that drives to anger in its thirst for justice, as we saw when Jesus cast out the money-changers from the Temple.[25] It has even been called 'erotic power', in its meaning of 'the creating, enlarging and sustaining of relationships'.[26] This is the power that at its deepest roots understands joy and refuses injustice, 'because the deepest liberation is union with others, and the clearest protest against oppression comes not from an abstract commitment to principles, but from the experience of suffering caused by oppression'.[27]

The clashing of these two notions of power haunts the Gospel stories, especially in the tragic fact that those closest to Jesus did not understand the profound difference being played out between them. Even at the Last Supper – in one account – they argued with each other as to who would be regarded as the greatest.[28] They never grasped the centrality of the way the kingdom of God meant the destabilizing of worldly hierarchies. Move to the Garden of Gethsemane, where ancient olive trees still flourish, where Jesus faced such anguish – and where the apostles slept. (There is an interesting tradition, captured by Fra Angelico's frescoes in the Abbey of San Marco in Florence, that Martha and the women remained awake and kept watch at the gates.)

On one level Jesus faces the terror of what is about to happen and the breakdown of understanding between himself and his close followers. There is also a tradition that Jesus – in his immersion in the cosmic battle between good and evil – suffered for the horror of all the evil that would befall his beloved city and by extension, all future sin of the entire creation. But the most profound level of the drama was the eschatological, the breakthrough from the historical struggle to the transcendent, where the dynamic of redemption as right relation, the dawning of the kingdom of God proclaimed by Jesus, would become the source of hope and renewal of creation, the trail blazed that all could follow. Even if immediate events would demonstrate the vulnerability of relational power and the fragility of non-violent resistance before the might of state power, this does not undermine the moral victory of the path of non-violence.

The anguish in the Garden – from which Jesus emerged resolute – ushered in his betrayal and arrest by Judas and his insistence that a violent response be rejected: 'all who take the sword will perish by the sword'.[29] Following the traditional Via Dolorosa, Jesus was then taken to Caiaphas' house in the Temple precinct and then to Pilate, the Roman governor. Here we are presented with the drama over Barabbas, the robber or bandit.[30] The fact that the people chose Barabbas – probably one of the Zealots or at least one of the social bandits of the Galilean hills referred to in Chapter 1 – over Jesus, is again illustrative of the dominance of violence over non-violence in people's imaginations. There is also a poignant wordplay going on. Barabbas in Hebrew means 'son of the father' – *Bar-Abba*. The mob has chosen a violent bandit over the real 'Son of the Father', Jesus. The contrast between Jesus and the bandits follows him to Golgotha, where he is crucified between two thieves.

This tension between violent and non-violent means is a dramatic contemporary issue. In November 2011 we witnessed protest camps against globalization across the world. Most of these were peaceful. However, one, 'Occupy Oakland' in California, gave rise to great concern and illustrates exactly the same polarization between relational redemptive power and the power of violence discussed here. As one participant reported:

To my horror, however, I observed and heard things that left me in a state of great concern ... The camp was ripe with hostility towards police. My conversations with the occupiers revealed little or any willingness to forgive and seek atonement from the police. Even more horribly, the occupiers seemed content to forget or even ignore the basic lessons our great non-violent leaders left for us. Dr Martin Luther King Jr said the most dangerous thing about violence is its futility. This great leader recognized that fighting violence with violent resistance leads to a continuing cycle of intergenerational trauma and hatred.

Yet many of the occupiers seemed ready for a violent fight – some welcomed it – and many more were unready to forgive. I fear this camp is in need of spiritual guidance lest it lead to the same horrible cycles history has witnessed many times over ... It is the lack of spiritual consensus and guidance that, I believe, is responsible for what I observed next.

The highlight of the day was a speech and a reading from the Egyptian movement that was followed by a 'Solidarity March.' The reading was disturbing to hear because its focus was on the justification for *violent resistance* ... What shocked me more was that no one (including myself) booed or hissed. We sat there and many applauded. Worse followed.

A leader of a Palestinian youth group read his own speech. 'Down with Israel,' he said near the end of a speech that focused on past wrongs. There was resounding applause. Then one of the leader's crew standing next to me said 'f.....g Jews,' and in the face of this I could stand it no longer. I told him that I believed it was racist to say that and that forgiveness and atonement is the only hope for peace in the Middle East. I told him that I forgave him and he should be careful with his thoughts and words. I told him that my best friend is Palestinian and I am close to many Jews and I wished sincerely to see the differences reconciled for the sake of the *innocent generations of the future*.[31]

The final act has now begun. Jesus is now condemned to be crucified and is on his way to the climax of his earthly life on Golgotha. His silence before Herod and again on this terrible journey illustrates that the choice of non-violent response cannot be understood by those who operate on the plane of systemic violence, and inhabit a universe where this is the sole ethos. Two incidents along the Via Dolorosa are important. First, that he is helped by Simon of Cyrene, an outsider, is notable. We hear nothing more about this figure – was he there because no disciple was forthcoming? Does this add to Jesus' experience of abandonment? Second, Jesus speaks with compassion to the women of Jerusalem, conscious as ever of their vulnerability:[32] yet in their understanding of relational power, it is women who stand with him at the cross. *There is still some faithful witness.*

The rock of Golgotha, Calvary, meaning the Place of the Skull, outside the city walls and end point of this journey, has been venerated since the fourth century.[33] From all possible features of this terrible death, two stand out for us: first, the forgiveness and promise of entry to the kingdom offered to the repentant thief – this, the very heart of Jesus' earthly ministry – show that he died as he lived, with the promise of healing on his lips;[34] and second, from the profundity of the experience of God-forsakenness issued that terrible cry, 'Eloi, Eloi, lama sabachthani?'[35]

How many prisoners in their cells share this experience of abandonment and forsakenness? It is not our task to ask if God actually did forsake Jesus – what is vital is that Jesus did not forsake God. His final words (as we are given), 'Father, into your hands I commend my spirit',[36] reflect the conviction of his early followers that Jesus' deep communion with God – from whom his authority and power originated – never faltered. A Trinitarian faith sees the Holy Spirit holding the dying Jesus within the unceasing love of the Godhead. That deep communion ushered in the resurrection.

The Via Dolorosa today

Returning to the Dominus Flevit Church on the Mount of Olives, we gaze on a deeply divided city, since New Testament times governed by succeeding empires – Roman, Byzantine, Islamic, Ottoman, British and Jordanian – all preceding the current Israeli government. Yet today's journey is embarked on with resurrection hope. Since the death of Jesus there have been countless crucifixions of the innocent in history. A new crucifixion of our times is the threat to the earth itself. Violence continues in new, ever potent form, especially in the threat of nuclear weapons. Torture is as alive as it ever was in Roman and subsequent regimes,[37] and Jerusalem has had its share of this.[38] In addition (as the introduction explained), this book has been written in the context of the Arab Spring and the continuing, even worsening situation of many Christians in Middle Eastern lands – especially for Syrians and Coptic Christians in Egypt.

The challenge is to re-embark on this ancient journey, marking not only the places of suffering but also the places of hope.[39] And it is also to widen these spaces of hope to include all groups in conflict with each other – to fail to do so would dishonour the redemptive project of Jesus, which aimed to reach out to all nations, including all in the vision of the kingdom. Before starting today's journey, let us note the sad fact that Palestinian Christians from the West Bank and Gaza – along with many Muslims – are prevented from coming to Jerusalem to walk the Via Dolorosa and celebrate Easter.[40] Yet Jerusalem is thronged with pilgrimages – many of which include Christian Zionists, who have little concern or interest in the lives of the 'living stones' of Palestine, namely, its long-suffering people.

So even if the journey from the Mount of Olives begins with the reality of the occupation and the memory of *Al-Nakba*, the catastrophe of the Palestinian expulsion from their lands, it also begins with hope of change. As we enter the gate of the city into the narrow Via Dolorosa, it is heartening to remember the broad coalition now from many faiths and secular groups who unite for peace. In England in June 2011, the House of Commons was addressed by Diana Neslen, from the organization Jews for Justice for Palestinians:

Thank you for asking me to speak tonight about Jerusalem. Tonight I speak for dissident Jews. Many of us feel existential pain when we discover what is done in our name in the territories Israel occupies. We hear about the Judaization of Jerusalem. That is no Judaization that we can recognize. When I consider Jerusalem, my first thoughts are of the obscene wall that snakes around the city, separating it from the residents of the occupied territories, denying them access and imposing restrictions on Palestinians.[41]

This stance invites us to walk the Via Dolorosa in the spirit of building right relation now. Yet as we pass the Ecce Homo[42] Convent of the Sisters of Sion (the traditional Second Station), with its magnificent view of the Dome of the Rock, it is impossible not to be conscious that this is East Jerusalem, the Arab quarter, and what this means today: 'Arab Jerusalem is languishing economically and socially because it is now effectively cut off from its natural hinterland – Bethlehem and Hebron to the south, Ramallah, Nablus and Jenin to the north.'[43] It may be fascinating to wander through the Soukhs – the old markets – of these narrow streets, with exotic aromas of incense, perfume, herbs and coffee (with cafés dating from Crusader times); but this should never blot out the reality. It is not only the barrier of the Security Wall, the daily oppression of the occupation, spiralling poverty, land confiscation and relentless settlement-building, but the horror of home demolitions that forms part of today's anguish.[44] As the former Latin Patriarch of Jerusalem, Michel Sabbah, writes: 'Every demolished home is ours, for why should we remain well-protected in the shadow of the tempest, whilst the poor, the weak, and the oppressed have to pay and to see their houses destroyed?'[45]

If Jesus reached out to the daughters of Jerusalem on his journey, so now women's groups are active in resistance, often across faith boundaries. So, for example, Women in Black began to witness against the occupation in 1998, and every Friday still protest in Jerusalem and other towns in Israel. Women in Black in other countries also join in solidarity. Bat Shalom is a group of Israeli women activists with a vision of peace. Machsom Watch, or Checkpoint Watch, is a group of Israeli women who monitor checkpoints in the West Bank and the military courts, in opposition to the Israeli occupation, claiming to have 400 members.[46] Checkpoints – notably Qalandia –

are the very public face of the occupation, causing daily humiliations and hardship (the shame of strip searches even for children), the separation of families, even husband and wife, prevention of reaching medical help and even being forced to give birth publicly at the checkpoint itself.

And finally we reach Golgotha, whose Rock today is enclosed in the Church of the Holy Sepulchre. This amazing church, for some the most sacred Christian site in the world, has had an eventful history, been the scene of many disputes, survived an earthquake, and is opened each day with a key by one of the Nusseibeh family, an ancient Muslim family with roots going back almost to Muhammad's time.[47] The location of the site of Jesus' tomb may have been preserved by some in the earliest memories of his followers. The burial cave, 'which looked toward the rising sun', was cut away from the surrounding rock and enclosed within an *edicule*, or 'little house'.[48]

It is a fitting place to end the journey, in the silence and waiting of Holy Saturday. In a sense, this is always the place where Christians dwell. Unlike Jesus' terrified followers, we have been nurtured in resurrection faith. Yet we still doubt and fail to act. Confronted by the contemporary anguish of those who walk the Via Dolorosa in Jerusalem and throughout Palestine and the Middle East, we keep the Holy Saturday of grief, anguish, yet silently waiting in hope.

Questions for reflection

1   What is your response to actively walking the Via Dolorosa, be it in Jerusalem or as the stations of the cross found in many churches with a Catholic tradition? Stay with those feelings for a while before returning to the beginning of the journey; this time walk the path alongside a Palestinian Christian who required a permit to enter Jerusalem, perhaps for the first time. How is this second walk different?

2   Crucifixion is a violent, bloody and humiliating form of execution. Take time to consider the non-violent nature of Jesus' self-offering, knowing the outcome for himself – if this is contrary to your understanding of the events of Good Friday, that is, as 'self-offering' rather than Jesus as 'victim', allow the proposition of *redemption*

as right relation to inform your musings. In what way does that help or hinder? Are you convinced that an ethic of non-violence is implicit in the life of Jesus and by extension that of his followers?

3   As we saw, Dominic Crossan suggests that in exploring the biblical narratives what we have is 'not *history remembered* but *prophecy historicized*'. This potentially challenges our reading of Scripture, especially in relation to how we then live within its truth – accepting a personal role as participant in the story or merely recipient of the same. Spend time reflecting on how you are changed by the way you read and/or hear the story of Jesus' final journey to the cross.

4   Meeting the needs of the myriad situations in our own times has sometimes led to a period of 'compassion fatigue', where it appears that people have ceased to care. The message of Jesus' dying is such that compassion for all is not an option but integral to the creativity and re-creativity of the Passion story, and beyond. What are the people, situations about which you feel passionately? Are you aware on what, or on whom, these are founded, that is, from where do your deepest desires come?

5   The faithful witness of those Christians, Muslims and Jews who engage in issues of justice with peace, peace with justice herald the coming of God's kingdom. If you are meeting in a group, spend some time discussing how you might learn more of their activities and, more importantly perhaps, what you might learn from them.

7

On the open road to Galilee

———•◆•———

Jesus, Miriam's child and Sophia's prophet, goes ahead of us on the open road to Galilee signifying the beginning of the still-to-be-realized *basileia* discipleship of equals.   Elisabeth Schüssler Fiorenza[1]

[A]ccording to the Christian Faith, this land is a 'Land of the Cross'. The cross awaits the Christian who wants to live here. The Christian must know that the tomb is empty, that the cross is still raised in Calvary, and that the glory of the Resurrection is to be found in his and her heart and faith and convictions and not in the external circumstances.
          Patriarch Michel Sabbah[2]

The Empty Tomb in the Church of the Holy Sepulchre is for many Christians the heart of the Old City of Jerusalem.[3] This church was called by St John of Damascus 'the mother of all churches', and tradition located the *omphalos*, the navel of the world, only a few yards from the tomb of Jesus.[4] It is very likely that the site of this tomb may have been preserved in the collective memory of Jesus' followers – 'Look, there is the place they laid him' belongs to the earliest Gospel text.[5]

The dynamics of Jesus' resurrection remain a mystery: apparently, the questions – How did he rise from the dead? What actually happened? – were not asked for about 200 years after Jesus' death. The heart of the scriptural resurrection message was: 'He is risen: he is not here; he is going ahead of you to Galilee.'[6] For the apostles, this must have been a sharp reminder of what Jesus himself had said to them on the Mount of Olives before his arrest: 'But after I am raised up, I will go ahead of you to Galilee.'[7]

In fact only John's Gospel takes the narrative to Galilee, to the seashore where it all began. The Synoptic accounts remain around

Jerusalem, with the exception of Luke's narrative of the journey to Emmaus.[8] The challenge for the pilgrim journey is to explore how to live *now* in Easter faith, in the knowledge of the harshness of the suffering of the Palestinian people, as well as that of the ongoing persecution of Christians in other parts of the Middle East.

For this, the final part of the Lenten–Easter journey, a three-pronged path is chosen: the meaning of the Easter message in the existential reality of Holy Saturday; the metaphor of 'practising resurrection' or 'living resurrection'; and the challenge to the worldwide Church to develop its prophetic dimension.

Easter's meaning in the existential reality of Holy Saturday[9]

The complaint is frequently heard that the Christian celebration of Easter skips too rapidly from the grief of Good Friday to the joy of resurrection morning. The significance of Holy Saturday is lost in a flurry of shopping for the Easter meal! Why wait, when we know he is risen? 'Why seek the living among the dead?' proclaimed the angels, as if urging us on. Yet in one sense Holy Saturday embodies a interregnum, a pregnant space, the truth of our contemporary situation of waiting for the fullness of the coming of the kingdom. It also recalls the credal tradition that after his death, Jesus descended into Hell to liberate the just souls awaiting his coming. I suggest that Holy Saturday is a metaphor for the present reality of Palestinians. As Melanie May wrote: 'Living in the light, the church is called to go to Hell.'[10]

The Church is always called to be present to those suffering places most in need of redemption, including the sufferings of the earth itself. Christians, living in Holy Saturday's paradigmatic stance of waiting and hoping, remember the three key messages of the risen Christ: 'Do not fear', peace and forgiveness. The three cannot be separated. First, 'Do not fear', 'Be not afraid', were words constantly on the lips of the earthly Jesus, fully aware of the dangers of the times but also the perils that would accompany anyone committed to full discipleship, prepared to risk life for the coming kingdom. Second, peace was his parting gift,[11] as well as the first word on his lips at his resurrection appearances.[12] But peace was linked with forgiving and being forgiven, the great ministry of reconciliation to which the entire Church is called by the risen Christ: 'So if anyone is in Christ, there is a new creation . . . All this is from God, who reconciled us to himself through Christ, and has given us the ministry of reconciliation.'[13]

We cannot avoid this core mandate: it summons all Christians to engage permanently with that movement of penitence necessary for peacemaking. But for persons and communities to engage with the conversion experiences essential for reconciliation, it is necessary to re-engage with their own painful memories.

Was this why Jesus recalled his followers to Galilee where he first summoned them to discipleship? This was not about a recovery of lost innocence. As Rowan Williams wrote: 'Galilee is the place where the past is recovered in such a way as to make it a place for the foundation of a new and extended identity.'[14]

Thus Peter, at the lakeside where he was first called,[15] is forgiven and given a new identity and authority by Jesus. The lakeside site today evokes this sacred memory. Through this forgiving love he is transformed – that is the kind of transformation offered to all in this journey of conversion.

'Practising resurrection'

This metaphor[16] encourages us to act out of resurrection hope and the transformation it promises as a present possibility, living as we do between Holy Saturday and the coming of the kingdom in fullness. The consequence of bearing witness to the ends of the earth is, as Patriarch Michel Sabbah wrote, that we become 'bearers of the resurrection in our vision and in our believing souls'.[17] And in our actions. Nor do the present sufferings preclude experiences of joy. It frequently shocks us out of our complacency to listen to the stories of those who, in the most threatening of circumstances – poverty, prison, serious illness – become 'surprised by joy', in C. S. Lewis' phrase.[18] This has all to do with touching the bedrock of Easter truth, experiencing that peace, forgiveness and freedom from fear that accompany 'practising resurrection'. Christians in the first centuries, although experiencing persecution, could still be joyful and practise a life-giving spirituality. Those who participate in non-violent action in Palestine practise this joy-filled spirituality daily – even though they have to confront fear and humiliation. Those who practise *sumud* by the Wall experience joy in the celebration of creativity and cultural theatre. Archbishop Elias Chacour from his Mar Elias college in the Galilee – a man who has lived in the shadow of this conflict since his boyhood – wrote his Easter message this year, in tones bursting with joy:

> Christ is Risen, He is Truly Risen!
>
> This is the only priceless gift we have and wish to offer you. It is true: He is risen! Come and see we have his empty Tomb. This is our religion. This is the Good News. This is the fundament of our faith. Because of the Resurrection we can call each other: brother, sister. Yes, because we accept to call each other Brother and Sister we can turn, all together, to the Heavenly God.[19]

I experienced a sense of this Easter meaning some years ago in a Peace Action outside Greenham Common in an effort to remove Cruise missiles from the UK. It was Good Friday and many Peace Groups were present in solidarity as we read the Markan Passion story together. There were armed soldiers to our front, behind the barbed wire, and arrayed ranks of police behind, to arrest anyone who put a foot wrong. Suddenly the snow began to fall – it was April! – and we sang, 'Be not Afraid'. This popular hymn recalls the Israelite memory of wandering in the desert, hungry and thirsty, yet experiencing the liberating presence of God. It was an apocalyptic moment. Living under this threat of nuclear weapons, in the reality of Holy Saturday, yet we could 'practise resurrection', experiencing already the inbreaking of a new world order.

Many individuals are inspirational in this process. If Easter is about recasting communal memories in order to enable a transformed present, then it is helpful to recall that there were Jews present in Israel before the Nakba who wanted to respect the rights of indigenous Palestinians. For example, along with others, the great philosopher and religious thinker, Martin Buber, was a supporter of a binational state in Palestine.[20] Following his original inspiration of *I–thou* relation,[21] he called for a dialogical consciousness. Among contemporary figures transformed by what Christians call Easter consciousness – apart from those previously mentioned – a Gazan doctor, Dr Izzeldin Abuelaish, must be highlighted. His story manifests that freedom from fear and refusal to hate that characterize 'practising resurrection'.

> On 16 January 2009 three Palestinian sisters were killed when an Israeli tank fired two shells into their bedroom. They were the daughters of Dr Izzeldin Abuelaish, a Palestinian gynaecologist, who, uniquely for a Gazan doctor, held a consultant post in an Israeli hospital. Abuelaish's book, *I Shall Not Hate*, is an account of his life up to this momentous event and movingly explains his remarkable reaction. In essence, Abuelaish, who likens hate to disease and communication to cure, has drawn on his medical experience to seek a new approach to the resolution of apparently insoluble conflict.[22]

Minutes after the attack, Abuelaish telephoned his friend, the Israeli Channel 10 News journalist Shlomi Eldar, to ask for help.

> By chance, Eldar was live on air. There then followed what must surely qualify as one of the most distressing interviews ever broadcast. We watch the face of the seasoned Israeli anchorman slowly collapse, as the news of the disaster is relayed to him by his Palestinian friend. Eldar holds out his mobile, switched to speaker phone, as Abuelaish's screams of despair ring out.

In reaction to this event, international condemnation of the Israeli incursion escalated and it finally ended 48 hours later. What is important for us here is the way Abuelaish refused to give way to hatred. (His wife had also died of leukaemia just before the Israeli incursion.) Realizing that 'violence begets violence and breeds more hatred', Abuelaish learnt Hebrew, developing what he believes to be the key skill of an effective doctor, namely communication: 'I talk to my patients . . . and colleagues – Jews, Arabs'. And he discovers that 'they feel as I do: we are more similar than we are different, and we are all fed up with violence'. His book concludes with his realization that his greatest personal and professional challenge still remains: to cure the disease of hatred. He does not deny the anger he feels about what has happened to him. Instead, he conducts it into a radical 'immunization program', which, as he puts it, will inject people 'with respect, dignity, and equality', inoculate them 'against hatred'.[23]

Another approach to revisiting memory, not dissimilar to Martin Buber's, is taken by Rabbi Michael Lerner in *Embracing Israel/Palestine*. Lerner calls for strategies of generosity to listen and embrace 'the other'. He wants recognition that Israel suffers from post-traumatic stress disorder (PTSD).[24] This condition is traced back through centuries of persecution and suffering, the experience of homelessness of the Jews, and anti-Semitism culminating in the Holocaust/Shoah. It remains an unhealed trauma: collectively Israelis cannot think outside this box.[25] Survivors of trauma, he asserts, 'create relationships in which they psychically reproduce the circumstances of the original trauma'.[26]

The link with the recasting of memory explored in the light of the Easter experience is that Lerner recognizes the injustice inflicted on Palestinians and calls upon Israelis to do likewise. At every point in history when a decisive action was taken, it *might have been* otherwise. Jewish settlers could have recognized the rights of indigenous peoples. Palestinians might have had some sympathy for post-Holocaust survivors and what now seems like a pathological need for security on the part of the Israelis. The point now is to understand that reconciliation begins with a movement of the heart and the transforming of consciousness, if we are to build a culture/political movement that helps people believe in the possibility of a world of love. This is what is meant by 'practising resurrection'.

The Church – called to renew its prophetic dimension and mission

It is very clear from all the examples given – a small proportion of what could have been said – that Palestinians, supported by some Israelis acting out of transformed consciousness, are doing all they can to achieve a just and peaceful solution to the conflict. The non-violent actions of resistance to the occupation continue on a daily basis. The Kairos Palestine Document has been written by Christians in Israel/Palestine, as a call to the world from the well of Palestinian suffering.[27]

But what has happened to the prophetic mission of the worldwide Church? The fact that there is a muted response – even though it is recognized that Israel is acting illegally in building settlements in the West Bank – prompts the question: Has prophecy left the Church? Does the Church live in that fear that 'practising resurrection' wants to banish? We in the West do not live in the face of persecution – yet Palestinians themselves have overcome fear in the face of daily persecutions. Is our timidity increased by fear of upsetting the Jewish community and being accused of anti-Semitism? But Jewish voices are speaking out, putting their lives on the line, being accused of being 'self-hating' Jews, standing up for justice and leading activist movements. Are we too enslaved by empire, whether the market forces of globalization or the superior power of military might? We follow a man who refused to take up arms in the face of the might of the Roman Empire. Have we allowed ourselves to be so consumed with post-Holocaust guilt that we are unable to speak the truth about the genocidal acts that the Zionist government now inflicts on another Semitic people?

Yes, truth-telling is hard, as Archbishop Desmond Tutu wrote:

> It has grave consequences for one's life and reputation. It stretches one's faith, one's capacity to love, and pushes hope to the limit . . . No one takes up this work on a do-gooder's whim. It is not a choice. One feels compelled into it.[28]

Concretely, this means many tasks and they are urgent. We are in solidarity with the work and commitment of ordinary people – so has it ever been with liberation theology. We work for the BDS campaign[29] because this is what the Palestinian people have asked us to do. Second, we engage in reading the Bible differently, seeking interpretations of difficult texts that are empowering for both peoples. Third, we engage with justice-seeking Jewish people in the search for a solution to the conflict. Together we will tackle difficult issues like the different meanings of 'chosen-ness', 'election', 'superiority' – and the image of God behind all these notions. Fourth, we challenge Christian Zionism in its fundamentalist reading of Scripture to awaken a vision of the just sharing of the land. And finally, we need to enter wholeheartedly into the vision of non-violence as the way to peaceful co-operation through a transformed Easter consciousness.

In this hope, pilgrims will keep walking the open road to Galilee, where it all began. Climbing the Mount of the Beatitudes that over-looks the Sea of Challenge is to re-encounter the universal call to peacemaking that heralds the coming of the kingdom. It also recalls for both Jews and Christians the vision of God's Holy Mountain, where 'the wolf shall live with the lamb' and there is harmony among all peoples, as 'the earth will be full of the knowledge of the LORD'.[30] The coming of the kingdom is a dream shared. To make this real – peace in the Bible lands – 'leaders need to have a vision, to have faith in that vision, and to be able to rally the people to share that faith'.[31] To incarnate this vision, Christians 'practise resurrection'.

Questions for reflection

1 Staying in the emptiness of Holy Saturday requires an inner accept-ance that Jesus has died. How readily are you able to stay within that 'pregnant space'? From your response, are you helped to understand those who live uncertain lives, especially those in Galilee?

2 Returning to Galilee is a return to the site of calling, of healing and of the foundational teachings of the Sermon on the Mount. Implicit in this, and in Jesus' post-resurrection greeting, is the emphasis on our being peacemakers. As you have journeyed through this book, has your understanding of what this requires been changed? Spend time reflecting on some of the stories in previous chapters of those engaged in active peacemaking, such as John Dear and Dorothy Day. What do they now say to you?

3 One of the gifts of the Spirit is that of 'joy' (Galatians 5.22). In today's complex situation in Palestine, where might moments of joy be found; how might you contribute to their increase?

4 Refusing to give way to violence, either that witnessed or that experienced, is a mark of humility and generosity of spirit. Spend time reflecting on how you deal with violence and/or unjustifiable anger, allowing God's Spirit into this reflection.

5   Christians in the Holy Land have much to teach us on practising
    resurrection. If you have not taken time to read the Kairos Palestine
    Document, then please take time now and then ask yourself, and
    your group, when shall we 'Come, see and witness' to further the
    resurrection of peace?

Appendix:
The Bedouin of the Negev Desert

Recent scholars have challenged the notion of the Bedouin as 'fossilized' or 'stagnant' reflections of an unchanging desert culture. In fact the Bedouin were engaged in a constantly dynamic reciprocal relation with urban centres.[1] By the twentieth century, much of the Bedouin population was settled, semi-nomadic, and engaged in agriculture according to an intricate system of land ownership, grazing rights and water access. During the 1948 Arab–Israeli War, the vast majority of the Bedouin in the Negev region fled to Egypt or Jordan: of the approximately 65,000 that lived in the area before the war, about 11,000 remained and were forcibly relocated by the Israeli government in the 1950s and 1960s to a restricted zone in the north-east corner of the Negev, made up of relatively infertile land in 10 per cent of the Negev Desert. Or they were forcibly displaced into the West Bank as refugees.

In 1951, the UN reported the expulsion of about 7,000 Negev Bedouin into neighbouring Jordan, the Gaza Strip and the Sinai, but many returned undetected. The new government failed to issue the Bedouin with identity cards until 1952, and continued to expel thousands of them. After the establishment of Israel, the Bedouin almost completely ceased to move around with their herds as a result of land confiscation by the state. Between 1950 and 1966, the new state of Israel imposed a military administration over Arabs in the region, and designated 85 per cent of the Negev 'State Land'. All Bedouin habitation on this newly declared State Land was termed illegal and 'unrecognized'. The government then forcibly concentrated these Bedouin tribes into the triangle of Beer Sheva, Arad and Dimona, and the Bedouin came to reside on just over one per cent of the Negev. Yet the Bedouin regarded 600,000 dunams (60 hectares) of the Negev as theirs, and petitioned the government for their return. Various claims committees were established to make legal arrangements to solve land disputes at least partially, but no suggestions acceptable to both sides have been developed. As a consequence, the Bedouin have lost access to their means of self-subsistence: many Bedouin men emigrated to newly established Jewish farms in the Negev in search of employment. However, they were not allowed to bring their families with them and were generally discriminated against in employment. In the 1950s, Israel began to extend mandatory education to Bedouin citizens as well as health care provision.

Many Bedouin have been urbanized, promised services in exchange for the renunciation of their ancestral land. Denied access to their former sources of sustenance via grazing restrictions, severed from the possibility of access to water, electricity, roads, education and health care in the unrecognized villages, and trusting in government promises that they would receive services if they moved, in the 1970s and 1980s, tens of thousands of Israeli Bedouin citizens resettled in seven legal towns – but these townships have become among the most deprived towns in Israel. The other half of the Negev Bedouin resisted sedentarization in the hope of retaining their traditions and customs, remaining in rural villages. However, in 1984 the courts ruled that the Negev Bedouin had no land ownership claims, effectively illegalizing their existing settlements.[2] Extreme unemployment has also afflicted unrecognized villages, breeding high crime levels. Since sources of income such as grazing have been severely restricted, and the Bedouin rarely receive permits to engage in self-subsistence agriculture, many unemployed Bedouin have turned to drug trafficking and prostitution.[3] Although they continue to be perceived as nomads, today all of them are fully sedentarized and about half are city-dwellers. Yet Negev Bedouin still have some goats and sheep.

Notes

Introduction

1 1 Corinthians 15.14: 'If there be no resurrection, then Christ was not raised; and if Christ was not raised, then our gospel is null and void, and so is your faith' (NEB).

2 Mark 1.14.

3 2011–12.

4 Dr Sabella, formerly a sociologist from the University of Bethlehem, is now working with the Near East Council of Churches. Quotation from John L. Allen Jr, 'Preventing a "Spiritual Disneyland" in the Holy Land', *The Tablet*, 21 July 2011.

5 Hamas is the Islamic political party: in power in Gaza, it also won the elections in the West Bank in 2008 but was rejected. It has been accused of violence and of refusing to recognize the state of Israel. Both these accusations are now repudiated by Hamas.

6 Gideon Levy, 'Netanyahu will go down in the History of Israel and of the World as a Forgotten Footnote', *Haaretz*, 26 May 2011. See <www.haaretz.com>.

7 Daud Abdullah, *The Guardian*, Monday 14 March 2011. Copyright © Guardian News & Media Ltd 2011. Permission granted to use Guardian copyrighted material.

8 Robert Fisk, 'Exodus: The Changing Map of the Middle East', *The Independent*, 26 October 2010.

9 Fisk's figure is possibly now too high: there are about seven million Coptic Christians in Egypt.

10 So wrote Anthony O'Mahony in 'Current Situation and Future of Christianity in the Middle East', *Living Stones Magazine* 36 (2011), pp. 2–5, an extract from Anthony O'Mahony and John Flannery (eds), *The Catholic Church in the Contemporary Middle East: Studies for the Synod for the Middle East* (London: Melisende, 2010).

11 Fisk, 'Exodus'.

12 O'Mahony, 'Current Situation'.

13 O'Mahony, 'Current Situation'.

14 All O'Mahony citations are from the online version of *Living Stones* 36, pp. 2–5.

15 Anthony O'Mahony, 'From Arab Spring to Winter', *The Tablet*, 3 December 2011, p. 5.

16 See Mary C. Grey, *The Advent of Peace: A Gospel Journey to Christmas* (London: SPCK, 2010). For the historical background of Christians in Palestine, see Introduction, pp. 3–12.

17 Grey, *Advent of Peace*, p. 122. This is a paraphrase of the line from W. H. Auden, 'At the Manger', from *For the Time Being: A Christmas Oratorio*, in *Collected Poems* (London: Faber & Faber, 1976).

18 Much of the surviving information about Egeria comes from a letter written by the seventh-century Galician monk Valerio of Bierzo, who praises Egeria and identifies her as a nun, perhaps because she addresses her account to her *sorores* (sisters) at home. Some say she was not a nun, on account of her freedom to make a long pilgrimage and to change plans as it suited her, the high cost of her pilgrimage, her level of education and her subject matter that focused on the sites and not miracles, as in letters we have by monks at that time. However, it is equally possible she was a nun, given the social constraints on married women of the time. Also, lone pilgrimages were rare among lay women at the time. Ignored by those who argue that Egeria was a lay person is the fact that she spent over three years on pilgrimage and was in no rush to return home, which would indicate that she was not middle class, but either financially self-sufficient or more possibly a monastic such as a *gyrovague*, or 'wandering monastic', as described in the Rule of St Benedict, who travels from monastery to monastery – <www.en.wikipedia.org/wiki/Egeria_(pilgrim)>.

19 T. S. Eliot, 'Little Gidding', in *Collected Poems, 1909–1962* (London: Faber & Faber, 1974), p. 222.

20 Some of these ideas on ethical pilgrimages are indebted to the Revd Pat Clegg, who leads regular pilgrimages to the Holy Lands.

21 PIRT = Palestinian Initiative for Responsible Tourism.

22 These reflections are the outcome of the work of Friends of Sabeel UK, Theology Group, *On Reading the Bible through Palestinian Eyes*, a group that I chaired. Copies are available via the office of FOS UK (c/o CMS, Watlington Road, Oxford, OX4 6BZ).

23 Julia Esquivel, 'I Am Not Afraid of Death', in *Threatened with Resurrection: Prayers and Poems from an Exiled Guatemalan* (Elgin, IL: Brethren Press, 1982). 'I Am Not Afraid of Death', published in *Threatened with Resurrection: Prayers and Poems from an Exiled Guatemalan*, by Julia Esquivel, 1982, 1994 Brethren Press, Elgin, Illinois, USA. Used by permission. To order a copy, visit <www.brethrenpress.com>.

1 The sea of challenge

1 John Greenleaf Whittier (1807–92), 'Dear Lord and Father of Mankind', in *Hymns Old and New*, ed. Kevin Mayhew (Bury St Edmunds: Kevin Mayhew, 1989), no. 116. Whittier was a founding member of the American Anti-Slavery Society and a Quaker poet.

2 Of course the emphases of the four Gospels are different.

3 Mary C. Grey, *The Advent of Peace: A Gospel Journey to Christmas* (London: SPCK, 2010).

4 Luke 9.51.

5 <www.en.wikipedia.org/wiki/Galilee>.

6 Resources for this section include: Andrew Ashdown, *The Stones Cry Out: Reflections from Israel and Palestine* (London: Christians Aware, 2006); Bargil Pixner, *With Jesus through Galilee According to the Fifth Gospel* (Israel: Corazin Publishing, 1992); Sabeel, *Reflections in the Galilee* (Jerusalem: Sabeel Ecumenical Liberation Theology Center, 2006).

7 See Chapter 3.

8 1,000–1,208 metres.

9 900–1,200 millimetres.

10 This alternative name derives from the Hebrew word for 'harp', *kinnor* – referring to the shape of the Lake.

11 Ashdown, *Stones Cry Out*, p. 20. Chapter 2 will explore environmental issues more deeply.

12 As noted by the author and by the Revd Pat Clegg.

13 Pixner, *With Jesus through Galilee*, p. 35. See also Bargil Pixner, 'Jesus' Routes round the Sea of Galilee', in *Paths of the Messiah: Messianic Sites in Galilee and Jerusalem* (San Francisco: Ignatius Press, 2010), pp. 53–76.

14 The Zealots were part of a political movement in the first century CE. They tried to incite the people of Judea to rebel against the Roman Empire and expel the Romans from Palestine by armed conflict. At least one of Jesus' followers – 'Simon the Zealot' – belonged to this movement and there was consistent misunderstanding on the part of the apostles as to whether Jesus would use force to oppose the Romans. Some scholars believe that the Zealot organization – in its politically active form – was developed later than the lifetime of Jesus. Sean Freyne, citing Richard Horsley, with whom he disagrees, uses the term 'social banditry' to describe a situation of socio-economic oppression that made the village people vulnerable and marginalized, and hence supportive of the bandits who fought for their rights against the oppressors. Freyne, though he thinks this is more applicable to Judea than Galilee, still believes there was a

level of poverty and a downwardly spiralling standard of living in Galilee. See Sean Freyne, *Galilee, Jesus and the Gospels* (Dublin: Gill & Macmillan, 1988), pp. 163–7.

15 It is now an Israeli National Park.

16 Matthew 8.5–13; Luke 7.1–10.

17 Matthew 5.1—7.27; Luke 6.20–49.

18 Pixner, *With Jesus through Galilee*, p. 37.

19 The Church of the Commissioning.

20 I referred to this in *Advent of Peace*, ch. 4, n. 48.

21 John Dear, *A Persistent Peace: One Man's Struggle for a Non-violent World* (Chicago: Loyal Press, 2008), pp. 48–52.

22 Dear, *Persistent Peace*, p. 50 (emphasis in original).

23 Dear, *Persistent Peace*, p. 51.

24 The Druze – of whom there are about one million in the world – are an esoteric, monotheistic religious community found primarily in Syria, Lebanon, Israel and Jordan. This community emerged during the eleventh century from Ismailism, a large branch of Shia Islam. The Israeli Druze are mostly in Galilee (81 per cent), around Haifa (19 per cent) and in the Golan Heights, which is home to about 20,000 Druze. The Institute of Druze Studies estimates that 40–50 per cent of Druze live in Syria, 30–40 per cent in Lebanon, 6–7 per cent in Israel and 1–2 per cent in Jordan – <www.en.wikipedia.org/wiki/Druze>.

25 The figures are disputed: the Israeli official number is 520,000; the UK Foreign and Commonwealth Office says between 600,000 and 766,000; there is also a larger estimate of 800,000.

26 <www.al-awda.org/faq-refugees.html>.

27 See Nur Masalha, *A Land Without a People: Israeli Transfer and the Palestinians* (London: Faber & Faber, 1997); *The Politics of Denial: Israel and the Palestinian Refugee Problem* (London: Pluto, 2003); Walid Khalidi (ed.), *All that Remains: The Palestinian Villages Occupied and Depopulated by Israel in 1948* (Washington, DC: Institute for Palestine Studies, 1992, repr. 2006).

28 See Elias Chacour, *We Belong to the Land* (Indiana: University of Notre Dame Press, 2001); with David Hazard, *Blood Brothers* (New York: Chosen Books, 1984).

29 See Sabeel, *A Time to Remember* (Jerusalem: Sabeel Ecumenical Liberation Theology Center, 2008).

30 From *Our Story: The Palestinians*, Conference Resources (Jerusalem: Sabeel Ecumenical Liberation Theology Center, 2008).

31 So wrote Walid Khalidi, cited in *A Time to Remember*, p. 47.

32 *A Time to Remember*, p. 48.

33 See Grey, *Advent of Peace*, pp. 83–4.

34 Ilan Pappé, *Out of the Frame: The Struggle for Academic Freedom in Israel* (London: Pluto, 2010), ch. 3, pp. 71–86. Also Appendix 1 on his own researches into the Al Tantura massacre, pp. 201–20. He stays in touch with survivors, as does Teddy Katz.

35 The Israeli Knesset passed the final stages of the *Nakba Law* on 23 March 2012, making it illegal for anyone to deny the existence of the State of Israel as the state of the Jewish people. As a corollary, any state funding for celebrations of *Al-Nakba* became illegal. Thus while Arab Palestinians in Israel are expected to commemorate the Israeli Independence Day, no provision can be made for similar celebration/commemoration of *Al-Nakba*, thereby denying Palestinians their history.

36 This is the most up-to-date figure I could find. Several sources still refer to 1.3 million.

37 These facts are taken from personal notes at the Sabeel conference in Jerusalem, 2008, where the position of Arab Israelis was referred to as 'handicapped citizenship'.

38 Jeff Halper, *An Israeli in Palestine: Resisting Dispossession, Redeeming Israel* (London: Pluto, 2008).

39 Halper, *An Israeli in Palestine*, p. 45.

40 Jafar Farah and the Mossawa Staff, 'The Palestinian Identity in a Jewish State,' in *The Forgotten Faithful*, ed. Naim Ateek, Cedar Duaybis and Maurine Tobin (Jerusalem: Sabeel Ecumenical Liberation Theology Center, 2007), p. 238.

41 For a fuller account of the situation of Palestinian Arabs in Israel, see Mossawa Center, *The Palestinian Arab Citizens of Israel: Status, Opportunities and Challenges for an Israeli–Palestinian Peace* (Haifa: Mossawa Center, 2006).

42 For example, Ched Myers, Richard Horsley – and especially Willard M. Swartley's *The Covenant of Peace: The Missing Peace in New Testament Theology and Ethics* (Grand Rapids: Eerdmans, 2006).

43 Ched Myers, reflections at Sabeel conference, Bethlehem 2011, personal notes.

44 Myers, reflections at Sabeel conference.

45 We know already there were critics of the Pax Romana even within the Empire itself, such as the historian Tacitus. There is an oft-quoted sentence from his life of Agricola, of a Caledonian (Scottish) chieftain from a conflict 2,000 years ago against the Romans that is still relevant now in the contemporary context of the violence: 'They create a desolation and they call it peace' – thus declaimed Tacitus' Caledonian chieftain before

battle. We know this critique of the Roman regime was the historian's own. See Tacitus, *Agricola*, trans. H. Mattingley (London: Penguin, 1948), p. 72.

46 Swartley, *Covenant of Peace*.

47 See John F. A. Sawyer, *The Fifth Gospel: Isaiah in the History of Christianity* (Cambridge: Cambridge University Press, 1996).

48 Aviezer Ravitsky, 'Peace', in *Contemporary Jewish Religious Thought: Original Essays on Critical Concepts and Movements and Beliefs*, ed. Arthur A. Cohen and Paul Mendes Flohr (New York: Macmillan, 1987), pp. 685–9; at p. 686 (emphasis in original).

2 Desert experience and the time of testing and trial

1 Ruth Burgess, 'Mark 1.12', in Janet Morley (ed.), *Bread of Tomorrow: Prayers for the Church Year* (Maryknoll: Orbis, 1992), p. 67. Reproduced by permission.

2 July 2011.

3 For the Temptation stories, see Matthew 4.1–11; Mark 1.12–14; Luke 4.1–3.

4 The translation of Nicholas King – *The New Testament* (Stowmarket: Kevin Mayhew, 2004), p. 89.

5 Greek = ερημος (desert).

6 Ched Myers, *Binding the Strong Man: A Political Reading of Mark's Story of Jesus* (Maryknoll: Orbis, 1998, 2008), pp. 125–6.

7 Exodus 3—4.17.

8 For the Negev Desert, see Michael Evenari, Leslie Shanan and Naphtali Tadmor, *The Negev: The Challenge of a Desert* (Cambridge, MA: Harvard University Press, 1971; 2nd edn 1982).

9 E. H. Palmer, *The Desert of the Exodus* (Cambridge, 1871), 2 vols, cited in Evenari, Shanan and Tadmor, *The Negev*, p. 27.

10 The current plight of these ancient desert dwellers gives great cause for concern – to which we will return.

11 Mark 1.13.

12 1 Kings 19.5–7.

13 Tawfiq Canaan, *Dämonenglaube im Lande der Bibel* [Belief in Demons in the Holy Land] (Leipzig: J. C. Hinrichs, 1929). On Tawfiq Canaan, see <www.en.wikipedia.org/wiki/Tawfiq_Canaan>.

14 Tawfiq Canaan, *Haunted Springs and Water Demons in Palestine* (Jerusalem: Palestine Oriental Society, 1922). Available at <http://commons.wikimedia.org/wiki/Tawfiq_Canaan>, and see also Mary C. Grey, *The Advent of Peace: A Gospel Journey to Christmas* (London: SPCK, 2010), ch. 4, n. 44.

15 Celia E. Rothenberg, *Spirits of Palestine: Gender, Society and Stories of the Jinn* (Oxford: Lexington Books, 2004).

16 What will become striking will be the language used by early Christians, of 'putting on Christ', 'putting on the garment of sincerity and truth' as contrasted with 'wearing the jinn'. Putting on the white garment of baptism takes on a special significance – clothing is seen as a symbol of fundamental change in life-orientation.

17 Malachi 3.1; Isaiah 40.3; Mark 1.11.

18 Willard M. Swartley, *The Covenant of Peace: The Missing Peace in New Testament Theology and Ethics* (Grand Rapids: Eerdmans, 2006), p. 94.

19 Here, though I agree with the views of Ched Myers and Richard Horsley as to the non-violent message of Jesus, I think that his message is more than resistance to the Roman Empire: it is political and yet more than political. As Willard Swartley says (*Covenant of Peace*, p. 96), it is difficult for contemporary exegetes to understand the full force of the spirit world in first-century times. Thus Myers sees Jesus' exorcism of the demon 'legion' (Mark 5) as liberation from the Roman army. Here – as the discussion on demons points out – I understand Jesus' vision of peace and reconciliation to include an end to foreign domination but also to point to a more profound vision that includes personal healing.

20 The second and third temptations are reversed in Matthew and Luke.

21 Matthew 6.9–13.

22 Luke 11.2–4.

23 Matthew 26.42, 45; Luke 22.42, 46.

24 See, for example, the gory tales retold by Simon Sebag Montefiore in *Jerusalem: The Biography* (London: Weidenfeld & Nicolson, 2011).

25 Stephen Grey, *Ghost Plane* (New York: St Martin's Press, 2006).

26 Matthew 5.5.

27 Matthew 21.1–10 citing Zechariah 9.9: 'Rejoice greatly, O daughter Zion! . . . Lo, your king comes to you; triumphant and victorious is he, humble and riding on a donkey.'

28 Matthew 11.29–30.

29 For John Howard Yoder see *The Politics of Jesus: Vicit Agnus Noster* (Grand Rapids: Eerdmans, 1972; revised edn 1994).

30 Matthew 8.5–13.

31 The film was based on the novel by Nikos Kazantzakis, *The Last Temptation* (New York: Simon & Schuster, 1960). The controversy was over the nature

of his relationship with Mary Magdalen: here my focus is the strong temptation to give up on his destiny.

32 Aung San Suu Kyi, 2011, <http://www.bbc.co.uk/radio4/features/the-reith-lectures/transcripts/2011/>.

33 Aung San Suu Kyi, <http://www.bbc.co.uk/radio4/features/the-reith-lectures/transcripts/2011/>.

34 See UNRWA, *West Bank – Area C: Herders Fact Sheet 2010*, <http://rhr.org.il/eng/wp-content/uploads/UNRWA-HERDERS-FACT-SHEET-2010.pdf>.

35 Carolynne Wheeler, 30 August 2008, 'Bedouin Nomads under Threat in Holy Land', <http://www.miftah.org/Display.cfm?DocId=17706&CategoryId=5>.

36 See Appendix for a history of the Bedouin in recent years.

37 Wilson Dizard, 2009, 'Water-Wars in Israel-Palestine', <http://dthrotarydrilling.com/News/10-Nov/Water-wars.html>.

38 Rosemary Radford Ruether, 2011, 'The Israel-Palestinian Impasse: Ethnic Cleansing, Ecological Pollution and Denial of Water: What Can be Done?', lecture given at the University of Winchester conference, Palestine Liberation Theology, 14–15 May 2011.

39 Dizard, 'Water-Wars'.

3 The Mount of Transfiguration

1 Tim McAllister, 'We'll just say that we've been to the Mountain', in *Caribbean Worship and Song*, Song 304 (Archdiocese of Port-of-Spain, Trinidad and Tobago: Liturgical Commission, 1997 edn), p. 172. Permission to reproduce sought.

2 Henri Nouwen, *Bread for the Journey: Reflections for Every Day of the Year* (London: Darton, Longman & Todd, 1996), p. 391.

3 Andrew Ashdown, *The Stones Cry Out: Reflections from Israel and Palestine* (London: Christians Aware, 2006), p. 32.

4 Of the three Synoptic accounts, we here mostly follow Luke 9.28–36. See also Matthew 17.1–9 and Mark 9.2–10.

5 Since 6 August is also the date of the atomic bomb explosion in Hiroshima, 6 August 1945, there is frequently great symbolic play made out of the divine light of the Transfiguration and the demonic light of the mushroom cloud of the explosion. This interconnection inspires many Peace Group prayer services and actions. I follow a different track here.

6 See <www.bibleplaces.com/mounttabor.htm>.

7 See Jeremiah 46.18.

8 Judges 4—5.

9 Source is personal communication from my colleague.

10 He recalls that antiquities and buildings remain from the Hellenic, Roman and Byzantine periods, so the site must have been inhabited for a long time since antiquity: as children they used to find a lot of pottery! Village people have oral tales going back to the twelfth century, when armed Benedictine monks dominated the summit of the mountain, especially during the Crusader period. They were besieged by Saladin forces and the Muslims took over.

11 In Hebrew the word can be understood as 'the Mountain set apart'.

12 Bargil Pixner, *With Jesus through Galilee According to the Fifth Gospel* (Israel: Corazin Publishing, 1992), pp. 97–8. The Hasmoneans were a ruling dynasty of Judea and surrounding regions during classical antiquity. Their kingdom ended with the Roman conquest in 63 BCE.

13 The date of the earliest churches on Mount Tabor is unknown. The Anonymous Pilgrim of Piacenza saw three basilicas in 570. Willibaldus, in 723, mentions only one church dedicated to Jesus, Moses and Elijah. There may have been three chapels joined together into one building, as in the present building. The current church was built in 1924 and belongs to the Franciscans.

14 Robert Browning, 'Bishop Blougram's Apology', in *The Works of Robert Browning* (Ware: Wordsworth Poetry Library, 1994), p. 439.

15 Annie Dillard, *Pilgrim at Tinker Creek* (New York: Harper Perennial, 1974), pp. 33–4.

16 See Paul Evdokimov, *L'Art de L'Icône: Théologie de la Beauté* (Paris: Desclée de Brouwer, 1972), pp. 249–56.

17 See the discussion on the work of Tawfiq Canaan in Chapter 2.

18 For this sociological approach, see John J. Pilch, 'The Transfiguration of Jesus', in Philip F. Esler (ed.), *Modelling Early Christianity: Social-scientific Studies of the New Testament in its Context* (London and New York: Routledge, 1995), pp. 47–64.

19 There are diverse versions of the story. We return to the Dome of the Rock and its significance later in the book.

20 The story is told in the Qur'an, 17.1.

21 1 Kings 19.

22 *Kenosis* refers to the 'self-emptying' of Jesus of divine glory to enter the full human condition. See Philippians 2.5–8.

23 Evdokimov, *L'Art de L'Icône*, p. 253; trans. Mary C. Grey.

24 2 Peter 1.17–18.

25 Neil Douglas-Klotz, *The Genesis Meditations: A Shared Practice of Peace for Christians, Jews and Muslims* (Wheaton, IL: Quest, 2003), p. 21. Reproduced by permission.

26 John 1.

27 Douglas-Klotz, *Genesis Meditations*, p. 43.

28 Douglas-Klotz, *Genesis Meditations*, p. 193.

29 David Adam, 'The Transfiguration of All', in Timothy Radcliffe (ed.), *Just One Year: Prayer and Worship throughout the Christian Year* (London: Darton, Longman & Todd, Cafod and Christian Aid, 2006), p. 217.

30 Thomas Merton, *Conjectures of a Guilty Bystander* (London: Burns & Oates, 1995), p. 157.

31 McAllister, 'We'll just say that we've been to the Mountain'.

32 I have already written on *sumud* in Mary C. Grey, *The Advent of Peace: A Gospel Journey to Christmas* (London: SPCK, 2010), pp. 85–7.

33 Habakkuk 2.2–3.

34 This is the Icon screen in front of the sanctuary.

35 We could cite Gandhi, Martin Luther King and others as manifestations of *sumud*.

36 Toine van Teeffelen with Victoria Biggs, *Sumud: Soul of the Palestinian People* (Bethlehem: Arab Educational Institute, Open Windows, 2011).

37 Toine van Teeffelen, 'The Story of *Sumud*', <www.palestine-family.net/index.php?nav=8-18&cid=17&did=4987> (lecture text from March 2008).

38 Mazin B. Qumsiyeh, *Popular Resistance in Palestine: A History of Hope and Empowerment* (London: Pluto, 2011), p. 235.

39 Toine van Teeffelen, Report of Arab Educational Institute's conference in Bethlehem, March 2012, personal notes.

4 Confronting the truth: A redemptive journey of conversion

1 Judith Gundry-Wolf, 'Spirit, Mercy and the Other', *Theology Today* 51 (1995), pp. 508–23.

2 The Lectionary for the Third Sunday of Lent allows the alternative reading of John 4.5–42 (prescribed for Year A) instead of Luke 13.1–9, the story of the Galileans whose blood Pilate had mingled with that of the sacrifices. It gives the opportunity to introduce the mission of peace as central to John's Gospel.

3 Donald Nicholl, *The Testing of Hearts* (London: Marshall, Morgan & Scott, 1989). Tantur is in greater Jerusalem, just outside the Bethlehem

checkpoint, clearly visible from its position, as is Har Homa, site of an extremely large Israeli settlement.

4 There are other sites but these are the most important.

5 John's Gospel does not mention the baptism of Jesus by John: his role here is more as witness to Jesus' being the Son of God – John 1.29–34.

6 After the Prologue, this part of John's Gospel – chapters 2—11 – is often called the 'Book of Signs'.

7 See Willard M. Swartley, *The Covenant of Peace: The Missing Peace in New Testament Theology and Ethics* (Grand Rapids: Eerdmans, 2006), ch. 11, 'Peace and Mission in John's Gospel', pp. 309–11.

8 Swartley, *Covenant of Peace*, p. 309. He cites as evidence of inclusion Isaiah 52—53, 56.6–8; Jonah; Ruth.

9 Genesis 33.19.

10 This is a variant Jewish tradition: the Bible says Joseph was buried in Egypt – Genesis 50.26.

11 A Christian church was built over the site. The well became popular for baptisms.

12 John 11.25.

13 Swartley, *Covenant of Peace*, p. 320 (emphasis in original).

14 This was the group, RENATE (Religious in Europe Networking against Trafficking and Exploitation), who are committed to struggle against the trafficking of women and girls.

15 See M. Grey, *To Rwanda and Back: Liberation Spirituality and Reconciliation* (London: Darton, Longman & Todd, 2007), p. 22. 'Step inside the church and what greets the visitor are stacked rows of skulls and bones, washed cleanly. By the walls are more sacks of bones. We were asked to be careful about walking in the church, as what is preserved here are the remains of 5,000 men, women and children, massacred on 15 April 1994. It is difficult to describe the effect on the group of seeing children's shoes, rosary beads, feeding spoons and rags of frayed clothing, all left as they had been on the day of the massacre.'

16 Norman Finkelstein, *The Holocaust Industry: Reflections on the Exploitation of Jewish Suffering* (London: Verso, 2000), p. 3.

17 Mark Braverman, 'Justice at the Gate', Lecture at FOSNA (Friends of Sabeel, North America), Conference 2009, <http://markbraverman.org/writing/justice-at-the-gate-the-role-of-our-faith-traditions-in-healing-the-holy-land/>.

18 Of his many groundbreaking works, see Marc Ellis, *O Jerusalem: The Contested Future of the Jewish Covenant* (Minneapolis: Augsburg Fortress, 1999); *Israel and Palestine out of the Ashes: The Search for Jewish Identity in the Twenty-first Century* (London: Pluto, 2002).

19 Rabbi Michael Lerner, *Healing Israel/Palestine: A Path to Peace and Recon-ciliation* (Berkeley: Tikkun/North Atlantic, 2003), p. xiv.

20 The latest incident has been an attack on his family home – three times, to date – by right-wing Zionists because of his befriending attitude to Richard Goldstone, the South African Jewish judge who wrote the UN fact-finding mission's critical report on the Israeli attack on Gaza (he later withdrew his comments).

21 Sara Roy, *Failing Peace: Gaza and the Palestinian–Israeli Conflict* (London: Pluto, 2007), pp. 19–21, at p. 21.

22 Jewish Voice for Peace, *From Gaza to Jerusalem: JVP Statement on the Escalation of Violence*, March 25 2011, <http://jewishvoiceforpeace.org/blog/updated-from-gaza-to-jerusalem-jvp-statement-on-the-escalation-of-violence> (emphasis in original).

23 The latter has now revised his opinions.

24 Ilan Pappé is now co-director of the Centre for Ethnic and Political Studies at the University of Exeter. See his *The Ethnic Cleansing of Palestine* (Oxford: Oneworld, 2006). It was Benny Morris who coined the phrase 'the New Historians' and revealed the extent of the refugee situation in *The Birth of the Palestinian Refugee Problem, 1947–1949* (he would later change his mind). Nur Masalha, also a historian-activist, is a Palestinian Muslim from Galilee, a colleague of the late Revd Michael Prior and editor of *Holy Land Studies*. He explains that his own views have evolved over the years. He is more interested in the role of theology and religion in the Israel–Palestine conflict, although beginning his 'political baptism' with secular activism. See also, *New Historians, including: Benny Morris, Avi Shlaim, Simha Flapan, Ilan Pappé, Tom Segev* (Richardson, TX: Hephaestus Books, 2011).

25 Hamid Dabashi, *Islamic Liberation Theology: Resisting the Empire* (London: Routledge, 2008), p. 255.

26 Dabashi, *Islamic Liberation Theology*, p. 255.

27 He is an Iranian scholar and founder of the Institute of Islamic Studies, London.

28 Dr Saied Reza Ameli, Institute for North American and European Studies, University of Tehran, speaking at conference, Towards a New Liberation Theology – Reflections on Palestine, 12 June 2005, School of Oriental and African Studies, London. See <www.ihrc.org.uk/activities/projects/7897-towards-a-new-liberation-theology-reflections>. His speech is available at <www.powershow.com/view/9d523-ZGUxM/Liberation_Theology_flash_ppt_presentation>. All quotes are from this presentation.

29 He cites the text: 'So whoever expects to encounter his Lord, let him act righteously, and not associate anyone with the worship of his Lord' (Surat Al-Kahf, Verses, 110).

30 Beverley Harrison, 'The Power of Anger in the Work of Love: Christian Ethics for Women and Other Strangers', in *Making the Connections: Essays in Feminist Social Ethics*, ed. Carol Robb (Boston: Beacon, 1985), pp. 18–19 (emphasis in original).

31 Rodolfo Cardenal, 'The Timeliness and the Challenge of the Theology of Liberation', in Mary Grey (ed.), *Reclaiming the Vision: Education, Liberation and Justice* (Southampton: LSU College, 1994), p. 21.

32 See Revd Naim Ateek, in 'Politics, Theology and Peace in Israel/Palestine', a lecture delivered at the Annual Gathering of Friends of St George's College, Jerusalem, 20 May 2010.

33 The Kairos Palestine Document, 'A Moment of Truth: A Word of Faith, Hope and Love from the Heart of Palestinian Suffering', <http://www.kairospalestine.ps/sites/default/Documents/English.pdf>.

34 I return to this idea in the next chapter.

35 Kairos Palestine Document (emphasis added).

5 Resurrection as re-creation

1 A sermon by Rowan Williams, Archbishop of Canterbury, at a Parish Eucharist at St Andrew's, Holborn, in London, on 7 October 2009, during which a new icon of the resurrection (painted by a sister of the monastery of Vallechiara) was blessed.

2 This is within the framework of a journey of conversion that the whole book explores.

3 Year A – but even Year C gives this option.

4 Willard M. Swartley, *The Covenant of Peace: The Missing Peace in New Testament Theology and Ethics* (Grand Rapids: Eerdmans, 2006), p. 303.

5 Rather, understand 'the world' as operating by a completely different ethic and way of relating than that of the 'community of the Beloved disciple'.

6 There are many attempts to explain the negative term 'the Jews'. It is clear it is not universal – Jesus and his early followers were all Jewish. It seems to indicate the period of tension and conflict when Christianity was separating from Judaism, which came to a climax in the fourth century under Constantine. From this period – and the declaration of Christianity as the official religion – emerged the long persecution against Jews and anti-Semitic strands within Christianity. See the helpful discussion in Swartley, *Covenant of Peace*, p. 281.

7 She died in 1980.

8 See Rosalie G. Riegle, *Dorothy Day: Portraits by Those Who Knew Her* (Maryknoll: Orbis, 2003).

9 Riegle, *Dorothy Day*, p. 90.

10 See Chapter 4.

11 John 20.19.

12 John 21.15–19. This church is believed to be on the site of Caiaphas' house – where Peter denied Jesus three times.

13 John 9.1–41.

14 John 9.22.

15 Jeremiah 38.6. This is discussed in Bargil Pixner, *Paths of the Messiah* (San Francisco: Ignatius Press, 2010), pp. 295–302.

16 John Hull, 'Open Letter from a Blind Disciple to a Sighted Saviour: Text and Discussion', in Martine O' Kane (ed.), *Borders, Boundaries and the Bible* (Sheffield: Sheffield Academic Press, 2001), pp. 154–77. Cited from <www.johnmhull.biz/letter from a blind disciple.htm>.

17 Hull, 'Open Letter'.

18 See Chapter 3.

19 Whereas John 3.5 does not say 'born again', the context is of a rebirth. See Nicodemus' words, 3.4, and Jesus' subsequent ones, 3.7, 'Do not marvel that I said to you, "You must be born again"' (esv).

20 Genesis 1.1.

21 See John F. A. Sawyer, *The Fifth Gospel: Isaiah in the History of Christianity* (Cambridge: Cambridge University Press, 1996).

22 Isaiah 6.1–10.

23 John 11.7–8. My paraphrase. There is a confusion in John's text (on the level of the final editor), since the anointing is referred to here, in John 11, whereas the Gospel does not tell the story until John 12.

24 Luke 21.37. The oldest house in present-day al-Eizariya, a 2,000-year-old dwelling reputed to have been (or that at least serves as a reminder of) the House of Martha and Mary, is also a popular pilgrimage site.

25 Of course there were two Bethanys! John 1.28 mentions 'Bethany beyond the Jordan'. Bargil Pixner is convinced this is Batanea in Northern Galilee and that there were connections between the two Bethanys. See Bargil Pixner, *With Jesus through Galilee According to the Fifth Gospel* (Israel: Corazin Publishing, 1992), p. 112.

26 Mark 14.3–10.

27 Brian J. Capper, 'The Church as the New Covenant of Effective Economics', *International Journal for the Study of the Christian Church* 2.1 (January 2002), pp. 83–102.

28 Morris West, *Lazarus*, Book 3 of the Vatican Trilogy (New Milford, CT, The Toby Press, 2005).

29 Fyodor Dostoevsky, *Crime and Punishment* (London: Dent & Sons, Everyman Library, 1911), p. 264.

30 Dostoevsky, *Crime and Punishment*, p. 267.

31 Dostoevsky, *Crime and Punishment*, p. 433.

32 Dostoevsky, *Crime and Punishment*, p. 455.

33 Duncan Macpherson, *The Splendour of the Preachers: New Approaches to Liturgical Preaching* (London: St Paul's Publishing, 2011), p. 136.

34 Rabbi Michael Lerner, *Embracing Israel/Palestine: A Strategy to Heal and Transform the Middle East* (Berkeley: Tikkun/North Atlantic, 2012), pp. 261–2.

35 John 12.1–11.

36 Mark 14.3–9.

37 Luke 7. 36–50. For Mary Magdalen, see Susan Haskins, *Mary Magdalen: Myth and Metaphor* (San Francisco: HarperCollins, 1993).

38 Luke 10.38–42.

39 It is customary here to refer to the work of René Girard, *Things Hidden Since the Foundation of the World* (Stanford: Stanford University Press, 1987). Girard bases his theory of violence on imitation, mimesis based on acquisitive desire. We want what everyone has and are prepared to kill to get it. This desire must be transformed into non-acquisitive desire by following Jesus as suffering servant for others. I disagree profoundly with Girard that violent desire is the founding ethic of the world, preferring a basis of divine relational energy, following Martin Buber and his idea of 'I-and-Thou'.

40 This discussion was begun in Chapter 4.

41 Luke 8.1.

42 I have written more fully on redemption as mutual relation in M. Grey, *Redeeming the Dream: Feminism, Redemption and Christian Tradition* (London: SPCK, 1989), ch. 5.

6 Walking the Via Dolorosa

1 Simon Sebag Montefiore, *Jerusalem: The Biography* (London: Weidenfeld & Nicolson, 2011), p. xxi.

2 Sari Nusseibeh, *Once upon a Country: A Palestinian Life* (London: Halban, 2007), cited in Montefiore, *Jerusalem*, p. 500.

3 Bargil Pixner, *Paths of the Messiah: Sites of the Early Church from Galilee to Jerusalem* (San Francisco: Ignatius Press, 2010), p. 303.

4 This painting is now in the Ashmolean Museum, Oxford.

5 The insight of Toine van Teeffelen, Bethlehem-based anthropologist. Source is email correspondence, November 2011.

6 David Roberts, 1796–1864, set sail for Egypt in 1838 and subsequently journeyed through Palestine. His – slightly romanticized and idealized – pictures have currently enjoyed a renaissance of interest.

7 Kay Prag, *Israel and the Palestinian Territories*, Blue Guide (London: A. & C. Black, 2002), p. 228.

8 *Dominus flevit* means 'the Lord wept'.

9 See Pixner, *Paths of the Messiah*, pp. 303–15; also <www.sacred-destinations. com/israel>.

10 Titus Flavius Josephus, 37 BCE–*c.* 100 CE, was a Jewish-Romano historian of Jewish history – an extremely valuable non-biblical source.

11 Matthew 27.55–56; Mark 15.40–41; Luke 23.49; John 19.25.

12 John Dominic Crossan, *Jesus: A Revolutionary Biography* (San Francisco: HarperSanFrancisco, 1995), pp. 124, 127. This was found in 1968 at Giv'at Ha Mivtar, in north-east Jerusalem, in a tomb dating from the first century CE.

13 Crossan, *Jesus*, p. 145.

14 Luke 24.25–27: 'then beginning with Moses and all the prophets, he interpreted to them the things about himself in all the scriptures'. It could of course be the other way round: that it was the process of combing the Scriptures that inspired Luke to write this sentence.

15 Matthew 9.9; Luke 19.

16 Mazin B. Qumsiyeh, *Popular Resistance in Palestine: A History of Hope and Empowerment* (London: Pluto, 2011), p. 234.

17 Qumsiyeh, *Popular Resistance in Palestine*, p. 117.

18 See Chapter 1.

19 Apparently there are now insufficient places for training in non-violence in Palestinian institutions.

20 See Chapter 3.

21 Qumsiyeh, *Popular Resistance in Palestine*, p. 235. As I write this chapter (November 2011), Mazin Qumsiyeh has again been arrested, then released, as part of a non-violent demonstration in the village of Al-Walajah. See also p. 48.

22 I have developed these ideas more fully in Mary Grey, *Redeeming the Dream* (London: SPCK, 1989).

23 Grey, *Redeeming the Dream*, pp. 103–4.

24 Carter Heyward, *Our Passion for Justice: Images of Power, Sexuality and Liberation* (New York: Pilgrim Press, 1984), p. 206.

25 Matthew 21.12–14.

26 Audre Lord, *Use of the Erotic: The Erotic as Power* (Brooklyn: Out and Out Books, 1978), cited in Rita Nakashima Brock, 'The Feminist Redemption of Christ', in *Christian Feminism: Visions of a New Humanity*, ed. Judith L. Weidman (San Francisco: Harper & Row, 1984), p. 64. Needless to say, this has nothing to do with the way the word 'erotic' is currently used.

27 Lord, *Use of the Erotic*, in Brock, p. 64.

28 Luke 22.24–27.

29 Matthew 26.51–52; Mark 14.47–50; Luke 22.49–51.

30 Probably this is not historical.

31 Source is personal email from Rabbi Michael Lerner, 15 November 2011. See the website of Tikkun <www.tikkun.org> for a fuller text (emphasis in original).

32 Luke 23.27–31.

33 During the 1973–8 restoration works and excavations, inside the Church of the Holy Sepulchre, it was found that the area was originally a quarry, from which white Meleke limestone was struck; surviving parts of the quarry, to the north-east of the chapel of St Helena, are now accessible from within the chapel (by permission) – <www.en.wikipedia. org/wiki/Calvary>.

34 Luke 23.41–43.

35 Mark 15.34: 'My God, my God, why have you forsaken me?'

36 Luke 23.46.

37 See <www.freedomfromtorture.org> – formerly the Medical Foundation.

38 Montefiore, *Jerusalem*, gives dramatic evidence of the violence that has played out historically in the Holy City.

39 My inspiration here is not only Sabeel, *The Contemporary Way of the Cross: A Liturgical Journey along the Palestinian Via Dolorosa* (Jerusalem: Sabeel Ecumenical Liberation Theology Center, 2008), but the way the Taizé community in France has acted in the last 40 years, to identify places of suffering and places of hope.

40 The permit system is complex, arbitrary and now extends to young people and children. Some even choose not to apply for a permit to visit Jerusalem because the system is so oppressive.

41 Diana Neslen, 'Building Peace and Justice in Jerusalem', House of Commons, 29 June 2011.

42 'Ecce homo' means 'Behold the man', and refers to Pilate's words – John 19.5.

43 Michael Hudson, 'Groundhog Day in Israel/Palestine', *Al Jazeera*, 16 November 2011.

44 See Sabeel, *Contemporary Way of the Cross*. All these brutalities are given moving liturgical expression.

45 Michel Sabbah, 'Eighth Pastoral Letter', cited in Patriarch Michel Sabbah, *Faithful Witness: On Reconciliation and Peace in the Holy Land*, edited and introduced by Drew Christiansen SJ and Saliba Sarsar (Hyde Park, NY: New City Press, 2009), p. 64.

46 These include former Israeli Prime Minister Ehud Olmert's daughter, Dana.

47 For a full history, see Raymond Cohen, *Saving the Holy Sepulchre: How Rival Christians Came Together to Save their Holiest Shrine* (Oxford: Oxford University Press, 2008). The Nusseibeh family trace their lineage back to the days of Muhammad.

48 Cohen, *Saving the Holy Sepulchre*, p. 3.

7 On the open road to Galilee

1 Elisabeth Schüssler Fiorenza, *Jesus, Miriam's Child, Sophia's Prophet: Critical Issues in Feminist Christology* (New York: Continuum, 1994), p. 190.

2 Michel Sabbah, 'The Mystery of the Palestinian Vocation', in *Faithful Witness: On Reconciliation and Peace in the Holy Land*, edited and introduced by Drew Christiansen SJ and Saliba Sarsar (Hyde Park, NY: New City Press, 2011), p. 166.

3 The site of the Garden Tomb on the Nablus Road, while a popular pilgrimage site, is not considered to be the tomb of Jesus on historical grounds.

4 See Raymond Cohen, *Saving the Holy Sepulchre: How Rival Christians Came Together to Save their Holiest Shrine* (Oxford: Oxford University Press, 2008), pp. 2–3. The story of the discovery of the tomb and the Holy Cross by Helena, Constantine's mother, is here well told, also the tremendous efforts to preserve it over the centuries for pilgrims today.

5 Mark 16.6.

6 A paraphrase of Matthew 28.6–7; Mark 16.6–7; Luke 24.5–7.

7 Matthew 26.32.

8 Luke 24.13–35.

9 See Alan Lewis, *Between Cross and Resurrection: A Theology of Holy Saturday* (Grand Rapids: Eerdmans, 2003).

10 Melanie May, *A Body Knows: A Theopoetics of Death and Resurrection* (New York: Continuum, 1995), p. 41.

11 John 14.27.

12 Luke 24.36; John 20.19–23.

13 2 Corinthians 5.17–18.

14 Rowan Williams, *Resurrection* (London: Darton, Longman & Todd, 1982), p. 35.

15 Matthew 4.18.

16 Melanie May introduces it in *A Body Knows*, but its meaning is found in many interpretations of resurrection.

17 Sabbah, *Faithful Witness*, p. 166.

18 C. S. Lewis, *Surprised by Joy* (London: Collins, 1998).

19 Elias Chacour, <www.twelvedaystojerusalem.org/chacour/pdf/lent.pdf>.

20 Bob Dufford SJ, 'Be not Afraid', in *Hymns Old and New*, ed. Kevin Mayhew (Bury St Edmunds: Kevin Mayhew, 1977).

21 Martin Buber, *Paths to Utopia* (New York: Syracuse University Press, 1996).

22 Iain McClure, 'A Cure for the Disease of Hate', Review of the Week, *BMJ*, 14 September 2011. The following citations concerning Abuelaish's book are also from this review.

23 Izzeldin Abuelaish, *I Shall Not Hate: A Gaza Doctor's Journey on the Road to Peace and Human Dignity* (London: Bloomsbury, 2011), pp. 101, 179, 197.

24 See Chapter 5, note 34.

25 Rabbi Michael Lerner, *Healing Israel/Palestine: A Path to Peace and Reconciliation* (Berkeley: Tikkun/North Atlantic, 2003).

26 Rabbi Michael Lerner, *Embracing Israel/Palestine: A Strategy to Heal and Transform the Middle East* (Berkeley: Tikkun/North Atlantic, 2012), pp. 207–8.

27 The Kairos Palestine Document, 'A Moment of Truth: A Word of Faith, Hope and Love from the Heart of Palestinian Suffering', <http://www.kairospalestine.ps/sites/default/Documents/English.pdf>.

28 Desmond Tutu, 'Realising God's Dream for the Holy Land', *Boston Globe*, 26 October 2007 – <www.boston.com/news/globe/editorial_opinion/oped/articles/2007/10/26/realizing_gods_dream_for_the_holy_land/?page=full>.

29 Boycott, Divestment, Sanctions. Rabbi Michael Lerner makes a distinction between *not* boycotting Israeli goods and boycotting goods from the settlements.

30 Isaiah 11.6, 9.

31 Sari Nusseibeh, *What is a Palestinian State Worth?* (Cambridge, MA: Harvard University Press, 2011), p. 193.

Appendix: The Bedouin of the Negev Desert

1 See <www.en.wikipedia.org/wiki/Negev_Bedouin>.
2 The Israeli government defines these rural Bedouin villages as 'dispersals', while the international community refers to them as 'unrecognized villages'.
3 This was supported by anecdotal evidence from Israelis who told me of their sons, reservists in the army, struggling with the levels of trafficking both of women and drugs among Bedouin (summer 2011).

Further reading

Scriptural resources

Bailey, Kenneth, *The Middle-Eastern Jesus* (London: SPCK, 2007).

Crossan, John Dominic, *Jesus: A Revolutionary Biography* (San Francisco: HarperSanFrancisco, 1995).

Freyne, Sean S., *Galilee, Jesus and the Gospels: Literary Approaches and Historical Investigations* (Dublin: Gill & Macmillan, 1988).

Kopp, Clemens, *The Holy Places of the Gospel* (New York: Herder & Herder, 1963).

Myers, Ched, *Binding the Strong Man: A Political Reading of Mark's Story of Jesus* (Maryknoll: Orbis, 2008), 20th anniversary edition.

Myers, Ched and Enns, Elaine, *New Testament Reflections on Restorative Justice and Peacemaking*, Vol. 1 (Maryknoll: Orbis, 2009).

Pilch, John J., 'The Transfiguration of Jesus', in Philip F. Esler (ed.), *Modelling Early Christianity: Social-scientific Studies of the New Testament in its Context* (London and New York: Routledge, 1995), pp. 47–64.

Pixner, Bargil, *With Jesus through Galilee according to the Fifth Gospel* (Israel: Corazin Publishing, 1992).

Pixner, Bargil, *Paths of the Messiah: Messianic Sites in Galilee and Jerusalem*, ed. Rainer Riesner (San Francisco: Ignatius Press, 2010).

Sabeel, *Reflections in the Galilee* (Jerusalem: Sabeel Ecumenical Liberation Theology Center, 2006).

Sabeel, *Contemporary Way of the Cross: A Liturgical Journey along the Palestinian Via Dolorosa* (Jerusalem: Sabeel Ecumenical Liberation Theology Center, 2008).

Sawyer, John F. A., *The Fifth Gospel: Isaiah in the History of Christianity* (Cambridge: Cambridge University Press, 1996).

Schüssler Fiorenza, Elisabeth, *Miriam's Child, Sophia's Prophet: Critical Issues in Feminist Christology* (New York: Continuum, 1994).

Swartley, Willard M., *The Covenant of Peace: The Missing Peace in New Testament Theology and Ethics* (Grand Rapids: Eerdmans, 2006).

Theissen, Gerd, *The Shadow of the Galilean*, trans. John Bowden (London: SCM, 1987).

Williams, Rowan, *Resurrection* (London: Darton, Longman & Todd, 1982).

Peace in the Middle East; Christianity in Palestine, Israel and the Middle East

Ashdown, Andrew, *The Stones Cry Out: Reflections from Israel and Palestine* (London: Christians Aware, 2006).

Ateek, Naim, *A Palestinian Christian Cry for Reconciliation* (London: Orbis, 2008).

Ateek, Naim (ed.), *Challenging Christian Zionism: Theology, Politics and the Israel–Palestine Conflict* (London: Melisende, 2006).

Braverman, Mark, 'Zionism and Post-Holocaust Christian Theology: A Jewish Perspective', *Journal of Holy Land Studies* 8.1 (2009), pp. 31–54.

Canaan, Tawfiq, *Dämonenglaube im Lande der Bibel* [Belief in Demons in the Holy Land] (Leipzig: J. C. Hinrichs, 1929).

Chacour, Elias with Hazard, David, *Blood Brothers* (New York: Chosen Books, 1984).

Chacour, Elias with Jensen, Mary E., *We Belong to the Land* (Indiana: University of Notre Dame Press, 2001).

Cohen, Raymond, *Saving the Holy Sepulchre: How Rival Christians Came Together to Save their Holiest Shrine* (Oxford: Oxford University Press, 2008).

Dabashi, Hamid, *Islamic Liberation Theology: Resisting the Empire* (London: Routledge, 2008).

Dear, John, *A Persistent Peace: One Man's Struggle for a Non-violent World* (Chicago: Loyola Press, 2008).

Dizard, Wilson, 'Water-Wars in Israel–Palestine', 2009, <http://dthrotarydrilling.com/News/10-Nov/Water-wars.html>.

Finkelstein, Norman, *The Holocaust Industry: Reflections on the Exploitation of Jewish Suffering* (London: Verso, 2000).

Fromkin, David, *A Peace to End All Peace: The Fall of the Ottoman Empire and the Creation of the Modern Middle East* (New York: Holt, 1989).

Lerner, Rabbi Michael, *Healing Israel/Palestine: A Path to Peace and Reconciliation* (Berkeley: Tikkun/North Atlantic, 2003).

Lerner, Rabbi Michael, *Embracing Israel/Palestine: A Strategy to Heal and Transform the Middle East* (Berkeley: Tikkun/North Atlantic, 2012).

Masalha, Nur, *The Bible and Zionism* (London: Zed, 2007).

Montefiore, Simon Sebag, *Jerusalem: The Biography* (London: Weidenfeld & Nicolson, 2011).

Nusseibeh, Sari with David, Anthony, *Once upon a Country: A Palestinian Life* (London: Halban, 2007).

O'Mahony, Anthony and Flannery, John (eds), *The Catholic Church in the Contemporary Middle East: Studies for the Synod for the Middle East* (London: Melisende, 2010).

Pappé, Ilan, *Out of the Frame: The Struggle for Academic Freedom in Israel* (London: Pluto, 2010).

Qumsiyeh, Mazin, *Popular Resistance in Palestine: A History of Hope and Empowerment* (London: Pluto, 2010).

Ruether, Rosemary Radford, 'The Israel–Palestinian Impasse: Ethnic Cleansing, Ecological Pollution and Denial of Water: What Can be Done?', lecture given at the University of Winchester conference, Palestine Liberation Theology, 14–15 May 2011.

Sabbah, Patriarch Michel, *Faithful Witness: On Reconciliation and Peace in the Holy Land*, edited and introduced by Drew Christiansen SJ and Saliba Sarsar (Hyde Park, NY: New City Press, 2011).

Schlaim, Avi, *Israel and Palestine: Reappraisals, Revisions, Refutations* (London: Verso, 2009).

Segev, Tom, *One Palestine, Complete: Jews and Arabs under the British Mandate*, trans. Haim Watzman (New York: Holt, 2000).

Sizer, Stephen, *Zion's Christian Soldiers: The Bible, Israel and the Church* (Nottingham: InterVarsity Press, 2007).

Zaru, Jean, *Occupied with Non-violence: A Palestinian Woman Speaks* (Minneapolis, Fortress, 2008).

Other miscellaneous resources: spirituality, poems, worship, story, environment, culture critique

Douglas-Klotz, Neil, *The Genesis Meditations: A Shared Practice of Peace for Christians, Jews and Muslims* (Wheaton, IL: Quest, 2003).

Esquivel, Julia, 'I Am Not Afraid of Death', in *Threatened with Resurrection: Prayers and Poems from an Exiled Guatemalan* (Elgin, IL: Brethren Press, 1982).

Evdokimov, Paul, *L'Art de L'Icône: Théologie de la Beauté* (Paris: Desclée de Brouwer, 1972).

Evenari, Michael, Shanan, Leslie and Tadmor, Naphtali, *The Negev: The Challenge of a Desert* (Cambridge, MA: Harvard University Press, 1971; 2nd edn 1982).

Grey, Mary, *Redeeming the Dream: Feminism, Redemption and Christian Tradition* (London: SPCK, 1989).

Grey, Mary C., *The Advent of Peace: A Gospel Journey to Christmas* (London: SPCK, 2010).

Haskins, Susan, *Mary Magdalen: Myth and Metaphor* (San Francisco: HarperCollins, 1993).

Heyward, Carter, *The Redemption of God: A Theology of Relation* (Washington, DC: University Press of America, 1982).

Heyward, Carter, *Our Passion for Justice: Images of Power, Sexuality and Liberation* (New York: Pilgrim Press, 1984).

Kazantzakis, Nikos, *The Last Temptation of Christ*, trans. P. A. Bien (New York: Simon & Schuster, 1960).

Lewis, Alan, *Between Cross and Resurrection: A Theology of Holy Saturday* (Grand Rapids: Eerdmans, 2003).

Lewis, C. S., *Surprised by Joy* (London: Collins, 1998).

May, Melanie, *A Body Knows: A Theopoetics of Death and Resurrection* (New York: Continuum, 1995).

Merton, Thomas, *Conjectures of a Guilty Bystander* (London: Burns & Oates, 1995).

Wheeler, Carolynne, 'Bedouin Nomads under threat in Holy Land', *The Daily Telegraph*, 23 August 2008, <http://www.telegraph.co.uk/news/worldnews/middleeast/palestinianauthority/2609041/Bedouin-nomads-under-threat-in-Holy-Land.html>.

Yoder, John Howard, *The Politics of Jesus: Vicit Agnus Noster* (Grand Rapids: Eerdmans, 1972; revised edn 1994).

Websites

www.aeicenter.org (Arab Education Center, Bethlehem)

www.bbc.co.uk/reithlectures

www.en.wikipedia.org/wiki/Calvary

www.en.wikipedia.org/wiki/Egeria_(pilgrim)

www.en.wikipedia.org/wiki/Galilee

www.en.wikipedia.org/wiki/Negev_Bedouin

www.lifesource.accountsupport.com/download/files/BedouinReport_May06%28095133%29.pdf

www.livingstones.org.uk

www.mendonline.org/NonviolenceRationalChoice.html

www.palestine-family.net

www.tikkun.org

www.unrwa.org

Index